Russian Life T

Bp. Herbert Bury

Alpha Editions

This edition published in 2023

ISBN : 9789357931717

Design and Setting By
Alpha Editions
www.alphaedis.com
Email - info@alphaedis.com

Contents

INTRODUCTION

My first inclination, when the entirely unexpected proposal of the Publishers came to me to write this book, was immediately to decline. There are so many well-known writers on Russia, whose books are an unfailing pleasure and source of information, that it seemed to me to be nothing less than presumption to add to their number. But when I was assured that there seems to be a great desire just now for a book which, as the Publishers expressed it, "should not attempt an elaborate sketch of the country, nor any detailed description of its system of government and administration, or any exhaustive study of the Russian Church, and yet should give the *impressions* of a sympathetic observer of some of the chief aspects of Russian Life which are likely to appeal to an English Churchman," I felt that I might venture to attempt it.

It has been given to me to get to understand thoroughly from close and intimate knowledge the commercial development of Siberia by our [Pg vi]countrymen; and yet everywhere, both there and in Russia proper, I have to go to every place specially and primarily to give the ministrations of religion. It can be permitted to few, if any, to see those two sides of the life of a great and growing Empire at the same time. This has been my reason, therefore, for undertaking this small effort, and my object is to give, as the Publishers expressed it, "personal impressions." I hope my readers will accept this book, therefore, as an impressionist description of Russian life of to-day, of which it would have been quite impossible to keep personal experiences from forming an important part. And though I write as an English Churchman, yet I wish to speak, and I trust in no narrow spirit, to the whole religious public, that I may draw them more closely into intelligent sympathy with this great nation which has seemed to come so suddenly, unexpectedly, and intimately into our own national life and destiny—and I believe as a friend.

HERBERT BURY,

Bishop.

CHAPTER I
RUSSIA'S GREAT SPACES

I will begin my opening chapter by explaining how I come to have the joy and privilege of travelling far and wide, as I have done, in the great Russian Empire. I go there as Assistant Bishop to the Bishop of London, holding a commission from him as bishop in charge of Anglican work in North and Central Europe.

It may seem strange that Anglican work in that distant land should be directly connected with the Diocese of London, but the connection between them, and between all the countries of Northern and Central Europe, as far as our Church of England work is concerned, is of long standing. It dates from the reign of Charles I, and from an Order in Council which was passed in 1633, and placed the congregations of the Church of England in *all* foreign countries at that time under the jurisdiction of the Bishop of London "as their Diocesan." It may be remembered that when the present Bishop of London went to Washington some years ago he took with him some interesting documents which he had found in the library at Fulham Palace, and which were connected with the time when Church work in the United States looked to London for superintendence and episcopal leadership. These he handed over to the custody of the Episcopal Church of America, knowing how interested that Church would be to possess them, and to keep them amongst other historical records.

The same rapid progress as that which has attended the American Church has been made in the Colonies and other parts of the world. New dioceses and provinces have been formed one after another, and in 1842 the Diocese of Gibraltar was formed, taking in the congregations of the English Church in Spain, Portugal, Italy, and Roumania, and all places bordering upon the Mediterranean and the Black Sea. But the other countries of Europe, to the north and in the centre, remain still, as far as Church work goes, where that old Order in Council placed them, in the jurisdiction of the Bishop of London.

It is impossible, of course, that he should attempt to meet this responsibility himself and bear the burden of such a diocese as that of London, and so the rule has been, since 1825, to issue a commission to another bishop, who, while being an assistant, yet has to feel himself fully responsible, and in this way spare the Bishop of London as much as he possibly can.

It will therefore be understood, as I have said in my few words of introduction, that, filling such a position and having such work to superintend, and also, for many reasons to be more fully explained in succeeding pages, finding the Orthodox Church of Russia very friendly towards our own, I shall write throughout with those whom I have termed the "religious public" very clearly in my mind and sympathies. At the same time I am hoping to interest the general reader also, and therefore shall try my utmost to give a comprehensive view of Russian life as it will be found to-day by travellers on the one hand if they give themselves time and opportunity enough, and by those, on the other, who have to go and live and work in Russia.

First impressions are usually interesting to recall. Mine were immediate and extraordinarily vivid, and were all associated with thoughts—which have gradually become convictions—of Russia's vast potentialities and future greatness.

When first I had the honour and pleasure of an audience with the Emperor of Russia—I will speak of it at greater length in a later chapter—one of the first questions he asked me was:—

"And what has most impressed you, so far, on coming, as a new experience, into my country?"

I was not prepared for the question, but answered at once and without the least hesitation—for there seemed to come into my mind even as His Majesty spoke, the vivid impression I had received—

"Russia's great spaces!"

"Ah, yes!" he said, evidently thinking very deeply; "that is true. Russia's *great* spaces—what a striking impression they must make, for the first time!"

Russia's Great Spaces—Winter.

I went on to explain that one can see great spaces elsewhere. On the ocean when for days together no other vessel is seen; on some of the great plains in the other hemisphere; riding across the great Hungarian tableland; and even in Central France or in the Landes to the west I have felt this sense of space and distance; but Russia's great flat or gently undulating expanses have always seemed to me to suggest other spaces on beyond them still, and to give an impression of the vast and illimitable, such as I have never known elsewhere. It is under this impression of vast resources, no doubt, that so many military correspondents of our daily papers constantly speak of the Russian forces as "inexhaustible." It is the same with other things also. They suggest such marvellous possibilities.

This is the impression I would like to give at once in this my opening chapter—a sense of spaciousness—power to expand, to develop, to open out, to make progress, to advance and grow. It is not the impression the word "Russia" usually makes upon people who know little about her inner life, and have received their ideas from those who have experienced the repressive and restrictive side of her policy and administration. But I can only give, and am glad of the opportunity, the results of my own experiences and observations; and those are embodied in my reply to the Emperor.

When I crossed the Russian frontier for the first time it was with a very quaking and apprehensive spirit. All that lay beyond was full of the mysterious and unknown, so entirely different, one felt it must be, from all one's previous experiences of life! Anything might happen, for this was Russia! "Russia" has stood so long with us in this country for the repressive and reactionary, for the grim and forbidding and restricting, that it will be difficult for many to part with those ideas, and I can hardly hope to remove impressions now deeply rooted. I can only say, however, that my own prejudices and preconceptions in the same direction disappeared, one after another, with astonishing rapidity in my first year; and now my spirits rise every time I cross the frontier of that great country, and my heart warms to that great people as soon as I see their kindly and friendly faces, their interesting and picturesque houses, and catch my first sight of their beautiful churches, with the fine cupolas above them with their hanging chains, painted and gilded domes, and delicate finials glittering in the sun and outlined against a sky of blue. Russia to me presents at once a kindly, friendly atmosphere, and others feel it also; for I have, just before writing these words, laid down a copy of *The Times* in which Mr. Stephen Graham—no one knows the heart and soul of Russia quite as he does, I fancy—writing one of his illuminating articles on "Russia's Holy War," says "People in Russia are naturally kind. They have become even gentler since the war began." Those who enter Russia expecting the unfriendly will find, I feel sure, as we have done, exactly the opposite—nothing but kindness and courtesy. It will be the same in other experiences also if I mistake not.

One of the chief difficulties ordinary travellers or tourists expect to encounter, for instance, in Russia is that of language.

"Isn't it extraordinarily difficult to acquire, and to make yourself understood?" is an invariable question, and certainly in long journeys across country, as from Warsaw up to Riga, and from Libau on the Baltic to Moscow, and especially in my Mining Camp Mission in Siberia, I expected to have very great difficulties; but, as so often happens, they were difficulties in anticipation rather than in reality.

Even off the beaten track in Russia any one who can travel comfortably in other European countries can travel equally satisfactorily there. Most educated people speak French, and an ever-increasing number—for English governesses and nurses are in great request—speak English. Great numbers of the working class speak German, the national language, of course, of Russia's Baltic provinces, on railway trains as conductors and in restaurants as waiters, and at railway stations as porters. Indeed, if any one is in the dining-car of a train or in the buffet or dining-room of a railway station or other public place, and has the courage to stand up and say, "Does any one here speak French?" or "Does any one here speak German?" some one ready to help and be friendly will invariably come forward.

In my first Siberian Mission, however, I found myself in a real difficulty. I had to drive across the Kirghiz Steppes from the railway at Petropavlosk, about four days and nights east of Moscow, to the Spassky Copper Mine, and the management had sent down a very reliable Kirghiz servant of theirs to be my interpreter; but I found that his only qualification for the work of interpreting was that, in addition to his own Kirghiz tongue, he could speak Russian!

For the inside of a week, travelling day and night, we had to get on as best we could together, and arrange all the business of changing horses, getting food, and paying expenses, largely by signs. Once only, and then in the dead of night when changing horses, did we encounter a German-speaking farmer from Courland or Lettland on the Baltic, and a great joy it was to him to meet some one who knew those fair parts of the Russian Empire where agricultural work brings much more encouraging results for the toil bestowed upon it than Siberia, with its terrible winter season.

Russia's Great Spaces—Summer.

But though to acquire a knowledge of Russian for literary purposes, so as to write and compose correctly, must be most difficult, owing to the number of letters in the alphabet—forty-six as compared with our twenty-six—and the entirely different way from our own in which they are written, I do not think it is difficult to acquire a fair knowledge of the language in a comparatively short time so as to make one's self understood and get along. I find young Englishmen, going to work in Russia and beyond the Urals, very quickly come to understand what is being said, and to make known their own wishes and requirements; and in a couple of years, or sometimes less, they speak quite fluently.

It always seems to me that the Russians pronounce their words with more syllabic distinctness than either the French or Germans. And that natural kindness and friendliness of the whole people, of which I have already written, makes them wish to be understood and to help those with whom they are speaking to grasp their meaning. This, of course, makes all the difference!

When the question of the great difficulty of the language is raised another remark nearly always follows:

"But then the Russians are such great linguists that they easily understand!" And it is usually supposed that they "easily learn other languages because their own is so difficult," though they encounter no more difficulty, probably, than any one else when talking in their own tongue in infancy. They are "great linguists" for the same reason as the Dutch—and that is because, if they wish to be in educated society or in business on any large scale, their own language will only go a very short way.

In Russia as in Holland, as I have been told in both countries, an educated household will contain a German nurse and an English governess, while French will be the rule at table. It used to be a French governess, but now the English governess is in great request everywhere in Russia and Poland; and, in the great nobles' houses, there is the English tutor also—not always for the language, but to impart English ideas to the boys of the family. When I was last in Warsaw, an Oxford graduate came up at a reception and introduced himself, and told me he was with a Polish prince who had astonished him on the first morning after his arrival by saying:—

"I have engaged you as a tutor for my two boys, but it will not be necessary for you to teach them anything—that is already provided for. I want you to be their companion, walk out with them, play games with them, and help them to grow up after the manner of English gentlemen."

There is no real difficulty, therefore, with the language, nor is there with the money of the country as soon as one realizes the value of the rouble, eight of which make nearly a pound, and that it is divided into a hundred *kopecks*, pronounced *kopeeks*, two of which are equal to about a farthing.

And now to speak of the actual travelling. Everything in the way of communication in Russia is on a large scale and in keeping with the answer I gave to the Emperor, and which I have placed at the head of this chapter. As soon as one passes the frontier, for instance, the travellers change into carriages adapted for a broad-gauge railway, and are at once in more commodious quarters. There is no land, I suppose, where travelling over great distances is so comfortable as in Russia for all classes; and it is incredibly cheap, first-class tickets costing less than third in our own country, for those using the ordinary post train, which every year becomes more comfortable and nearer to the standard of the wagon-lit. There are excellent lavatories, kept perfectly clean, where one can wash, shave, and almost have a sponge bath, for—though without the luxuries of the Trans-Siberian express—there is more room.

There is usually a restaurant-car on the long-distance trains—and practically all the trains in Russia are for long distances—and, if not, there is plenty of time to get food at the stations on the way. Conductors will take every care and trouble to get what is necessary, and first and second-class compartments are never overcrowded, as far as my experience goes. I believe, indeed, that not more than four people may be put into a compartment for the night, and, as the cushioned back of the seats can be lifted up, all the four travellers can be sure of being able to lie down. The first-class compartments on a post train are divided into two by folding-doors, and one is allowed to buy a *platzcarte* and so have the whole compartment to one's self. Every accommodation too is provided for lying down comfortably in the third-class, and the travellers there are always the happiest-looking on the train.

Another consideration shown to the public is that the scale of charges falls in proportion to the distance to be traversed. The stations are specially spacious, particularly along the routes beyond Moscow, where emigration continually goes on into the great pastoral lands of Siberia. In the summer months the traffic is very great, and it is one of the most touching and appealing experiences I can recall to pass through one of the great waiting-halls of such a station as Samara, at night, and pick one's way amongst the sleeping families of peasants waiting to get their connection with another line, and resting in the meantime. Their little possessions are all about them, and father and mother and sons and daughters lie gathered close up together, pillowing their heads upon each other, good-looking, prettily dressed, and fast asleep—as attractive a picture as any one could wish to see.

There is a great freedom of movement everywhere in Russia, and I do not remember having seen the word *verboten* (the German for "forbidden"), or its equivalent, in any part of a Russian or Siberian station. The rule of having three bells to announce approaching departure is a most excellent one, whether the pause is long or short, the first ringing very audibly about five minutes, the second one minute, and the third immediately before departure. If travelling long distances, the ten-minutes' stop at all large towns gives plenty of opportunity for exercise and fresh air, and the absolute certainty of hearing the bells gives a perfect sense of security that no one will be left behind. If the bell rings twice just as the train enters the station, every one knows that the stay will be short, and that it is not worth while getting out.

Some of the most resting and refreshing experiences I have ever had have been those of travelling day after day for some two or three thousand miles in Russia, getting one's correspondence straight, for writing is quite easy in those steady and slow-moving express trains, reading up reviews and periodicals or making plans for future journeys, looking out of the windows in the early morning or late evening, all varied by meals in the *coupé* or at a station, seeing all kinds of interesting people in strange costumes, and many attractive incidents at places where one alights for a walk and exercise.

More interesting than the railways, however, are the rivers. How large these are, and how important a part they have filled in the past, before the days of railways, and still play in the commerce and life of the people, will be seen at once by a glance at the map at the end of the book. None of them, however, though one gets a real affection for the Neva after sledging over it in the winter and sailing upon it in the summer, attracts and indeed fascinates, as the Volga never fails to do. It is magnificent in size, and is the largest in Europe, 2,305 miles in length, three times as long as the Rhine. Many of us know what the Rhine is to the Germans. Treitschke, as we have been reminded in one of the most widely read of modern books, when leaving Bonn, wrote to a friend, "To-morrow I shall see the Rhine for the last time. The memory of that noble river will keep my heart pure, and save me from sad and evil thoughts throughout all the days of my life."

I have always understood the strong appeal to the historic, and even the poetic, sense which the Rhine puts forth, but I never understood the sense of the ideal which a river might convey until I saw, approached, and crossed the Volga.

It was a May evening, three years ago, as we drew near and then passed along its right bank before crossing. It was of the loveliest colour of rich and living brown, like that of a healthy human skin, carrying life and burdens of every description upon its ample bosom, fostering all kinds of enterprise and activity on its shores, and flowing on with stately dignity, as if it would not be hurried from its calm consciousness of its own strength and significance for those nine provinces through which it passes on its way to the Caspian. I felt its spell at once, and, as I crossed the great bridge over which the Trans-Siberian line is carried—an exquisite piece of engineering a mile and a quarter in length—I knew that I should always feel a curious sense of personality in connection with that glorious river. I think Merriman, in one of his novels, speaks of associating a sense of consciousness with the Volga; and that is just what I have felt each time of crossing over its bounteous-looking, calm, and steady flow. It seems to live and know.

The third and last "difficulty" which I will speak of in this opening chapter, and which is no difficulty at all, is the passport. Every one in Russia must possess one; and, if travelling and intending to spend one or two nights in a place, it must be sent to the proper official and be duly stamped. It must be *visèd* by the Russian ambassador, or minister, at the place from which one starts before entering Russia; and, which is even more important, it must be *visèd* by the right official at some important town or place of government, and stamped with the necessary permission, before one is able to *leave* Russia.

It is natural to feel at the frontier, when entering the country, "I hope it is all right," as the passport is handed to the customs officer, and, with just a little approach to anxious uncertainty, after all one has heard and read; but it is almost impossible to avoid real anxiety that it will be found correct and in order as it is presented at the frontier when *leaving*, as the difficulties of being kept back there, so far away from the great cities, would be far greater than those of being refused *admission* from some technicality that could probably be put right by a telegram to and from England.

"But surely the passport must prevent you from feeling that sense of freedom that you have spoken of more than once—surely *that* must give a sense of repression and suspicion and being watched and having an eye kept on your doings," my reader will be thinking, and perhaps many other people have the same feeling. It is, however, exactly the opposite with me, for my passport in Russia and Siberia is a great stand-by, and gives me a great sense of being always able to establish my own identity.

There can be little doubt that the passport was established from the first in the interests of the community, for it is entirely in their own interests that people should possess them. No one who is honest in purpose can have any difficulty in procuring one or be brought to any trouble through it. The necessity of frequently producing them, in moving from place to place, is always in the interests of the traveller in a vast empire like Russia. It has given me a great feeling of confidence in launching out, as has been necessary now and then, into the unknown, to feel "They will be able to trace me all along by the entries made in official registers, as the passport has been stamped." If any one disappeared in Russia the police would be able to trace his movements to very near the place of disappearance.

It is a great help in getting letters also to have a passport, for we are just as anxious as the officials can be that our letters should not go to the wrong people; and in travelling in out-of-the-way places it is simply invaluable in getting the help, advice, and recognition that sometimes are so very necessary. Even the passport, therefore, helps to deepen the sense of security and freedom with which one launches out into Russian travel, anxious to gain all that it has to give in information and stimulating experience.

It will be remembered, however, that I speak always not as a resident, but as a traveller; and there is just this difference—*indeed, it is a vast difference*— between my own opportunities and those of an ordinary traveller. Travelling as the bishop for the English Church work in Russia, in every place our clergy and residents have only been too happy to speak of their own experiences and impressions, some of them lifelong and all-important. When travelling in Siberia, and the guest from time to time of managers of the great mines, I go out with them day after day and get long conversations with them, their wives, and members of the staff. I hear all about early struggles, hopes and fears, difficulties and triumphs extending over many years. The conditions of life and characteristics of the people in vast tracts of country are described to me by those who know them well. No one but a bishop travelling through the country would have the same information so freely volunteered to him. And it is this which has led me to feel that I might, without undue presumption, write for ordinary readers about the life of a country in which I have not, as yet, spent a great many years.

It *is* a great country, as all we who know it feel, and "It doth not yet appear what it shall be." If some of us are right in thinking of the Russians as a great race with a vast country of tremendous resources; who can in any way picture the great and wonderful possibilities of their future? It will be my task to try and show how little opportunity they have had as yet of getting their share of modern civilization, how imperfectly, as yet, the ethical side of their religion has been imparted to them; and still, in spite of all this and of other defects of their social and religious life, how much they have accomplished in the way of real achievement.

I fail to see how any one can help feeling the greatest interest—hopeful and expectant—about their future, or feel anything else but the great thankfulness that I feel myself, that we and they as peoples have been brought so intimately together by circumstances which few could have foreseen only a very few years ago, but which have come about not only, as some would say, in the course of Providence, but in a very true sense, as I trust our and their national histories shall show in time to come, "According to the good hand of our GOD upon us."

The Kremlin.

CHAPTER II
GENERAL SOCIAL LIFE

The whole life of the Russian people reminds those who visit them continually and in every possible way that they are in a religious country; for everywhere there is the *ikon*, or sacred religious picture. There are other ways, especially the columns of the newspapers full of notices of private and public ministrations and pathetic requests for prayers for the departed, of bringing religion continually before the public mind, but the *ikon* is most in evidence. It is a picture in one sense, for it is a representation either of our LORD or of the Holy Virgin or of some well-known saint; but the garments are in relief, often composed of one of the precious metals and ornamented in some cases with jewels; and thus it is quite different from other sacred pictures. It is the first characteristic evidence of "Russia" to meet one's eyes on entering, and the last to be seen as one leaves, any public place.

"A great picture of the Virgin and Child hangs in the custom-house at Wirballen," writes Mr. Rothay Reynolds at the beginning of *My Russian Year*, "with a little lamp flickering before it."

"The foreigner, who was a few minutes before on the German side of the frontier and stands on Russian soil for the first time, looks at the shrine with curiosity. Porters are hurrying in with luggage, and travellers are chattering in half a dozen languages. An official at a desk in the middle of the great hall is examining passports. A man is protesting that he did not know that playing-cards were contraband; a woman is radiant, for the dirty lining she has sewn in a new Paris hat has deceived the inquisitors. Everybody is in a hurry to be through with the business, and free to lunch in the adjoining restaurant before going on to St. Petersburg. It is a strange home for the majestic Virgin of the Byzantine picture.

"Here, at the threshold of the empire, Russia placards—S. Paul's vivid Greek gives me the word—her faith before the eyes of all comers. In the bustle of a custom-house, charged with fretfulness and impatience and meanness, Russia sets forth her belief in a life beyond the grave and her conviction that the ideals presented by the picture are the noblest known to mankind."

Nowhere as in Russia is one reminded so constantly, in what we should consider most unlikely places, that we are in a Christian country. In the streets and at railway stations, in baths, hotels, post offices, shops, and warehouses, in the different rooms of factories and workshops, in private houses, rich and poor alike, in government houses, and even in places of evil resort which I will not specify, as well as in prisons, indeed in *every* public place there is the *ikon*—most frequently representing the Holy Mother and Child—and its lamp burning before it.

In later chapters I will write more at length upon religion and worship, but I must give the reader *at once*, if a stranger to Russia, something of the impression which the ubiquity of the *ikon* makes upon those who go there for the first time. It is *always* to be seen. And though I will try and describe what it directly represents in the shape of Church life later, yet from the very first I must write, as it were, with the *ikon* before me. I must see with my mind's eye the Holy Mother clasping the Divine Child to her bosom, with a few flowers and a twinkling little light before them, all the time I write, whether it is of things secular or sacred, grave or gay, national or international, or I shall give out but little of the spirit which I feel I have breathed deeply into my life in that wonderful country, and certainly shall not be able to help any reader who has not been there as yet to understand why it should be spoken of as "Holy Russia."

That which the *ikon* stands for, therefore, must be the spirit of every chapter I write, or I shall give my readers no true picture of Russian life.

Fortunately for those who want further particulars than such a book as this can give them—and it will fail in its purpose if it does not make many readers *wish* to have them—there has been a very excellent *Baedeker's Guide to Russia* published last year, which is a wonderfully complete work considering the vast empire with which it has to deal. I will therefore attempt nothing at all in the way of statistics or descriptions such as a guide-book gives, or such as will be found in the excellent books to which I shall often refer. If I can take my readers with me in thought as I travel about Russia and Siberia, and can give them some of the information which has been given so freely to me, and can convey to them some portion of the impressions made upon me when far away from the beaten track, and above all can lead them to give their sympathies freely and generously to the people of the land and to our own countrymen so hospitably welcomed amongst them, and so generously treated, I shall be more than repaid for my work, and shall ask nothing better.

In Russia there are two forms of government, clearly and strenuously at work, and wide asunder in their character, the autocratic and the democratic. It is impossible to do much more than mention these two tremendous forces, which are so strongly forming the character, and determining the destinies for a long time to come, of a great people.

Since 1905 the Russian Empire has had constitutional government under the form of an Imperial Council or First Chamber, the Imperial Duma or Second Chamber, with the Emperor, advised by a small council of ministers, still an autocratic sovereign. The Emperor can overrule any legislation, and probably would if advised by a unanimous council; but it must be evident to most people if they think a little, that even now he would be very reluctant to do this except in some very grave crisis of the national life, and that in time to come he will never dream of such interference. Constitutional government in Russia has really begun, and when one considers the past it is clear that great progress has been made in the direction of constitutional freedom since it was granted in 1905. The reconstitution of the Polish nation, the stirring amongst the Finns, the rising hopes of the Jews, the national aspirations of Mongolia more and more fully expressed, the general "moving upon the face of the waters" of the Spirit which makes a free people, cannot but rivet the attention of those interested in social and national life upon Russia at this time, when the autocratic government of long standing is passing, so simply and so naturally, it would seem, into the constitutional.

Since the emancipation of the serfs there has been a steady growth of the democratic, almost communal, spirit in all the peasant villages of Russia, and though their powers have been somewhat curtailed since 1889 they are self-governing and very responsible communities. Some of the best and most interesting Russian stories, therefore, deal with incidents and experiences in village life; and it is the great fact that Sir Donald Mackenzie Wallace, whose book upon Russia is one of the most complete character, went and shut himself out from the rest of the world at the little village of Ivanofka, in the province of Novgorod, and there drank in the spirit of the language and of the national life, that makes his compendious work a real classic for those who want truly to understand Russian life and nationality.

There are two distinct social and constitutional forces at work, therefore, and not working slowly and deliberately, as so often in the past, but with great rapidity—the autocratic seeking to realize its responsibilities and to fulfil them, and the democratic feeling that its ideals are coming nearer to being realized every day.

There is consequently no country so absorbingly interesting to the constitutionalist at this time as Russia. Nothing can be more stimulating, to those who want to read the signs of the times, than to know that revolutionaries, such as M. Bourtzeff,[1] who had left their country in despair to plan and plot, have now returned, without troubling whether they would be pardoned or punished, full of expectant hope for their country's constitutional future. Perhaps cautious people will hope that progress may be slow, but the great thing is to be able to say, "It moves."

Every city and great town in Russia has something specially characteristic about it, and of course they are, as yet, very few in number. Catherine the Great, as is well known, thought cities and towns could be created, though she found out her mistake, and Russia still remains a land of villages rather than of towns, but the great towns which do exist have usually very distinctive features.

Petrograd, for instance, though, as Peter intended it should be, essentially modern, has its very special features in its domed churches and the magnificence of its wide river with the great palaces upon its banks and bordering upon its quays. The fortress of S. Peter and S. Paul, on the opposite side, "home of political prisoners and dead Tsars," when the sun is setting, is never to be forgotten, and enters at once upon the field of vision as one thinks of Peter's capital.

Then Moscow! How well I remember Bishop Creighton's enthusiasm whenever he spoke of Moscow. Though his face might be calm and its expression grave before, only let Moscow be mentioned and it would light up at once, as with sparkling eyes he would exclaim:—

"Moscow!—oh, you must see Moscow: nothing in the world is like it. You *must* see it."

But it is really the Kremlin which makes Moscow unique, with an intangible influence and sense of association connected with it that no one can describe, as one thinks of its historic past and of Napoleon! The Kremlin! I had read and heard descriptions of it from time to time, but was in no way prepared for that vast area of palaces, churches, treasuries, great houses, and barracks, enclosed by glorious walls and towers and entered by impressive gateways, over which one gazed with wondering eyes when seen first under the blue sky and brilliant winter sun.

The Gate of the Redeemer, Moscow.

It is no use attempting to describe it; but Moscow is the Kremlin, and to *feel* the Kremlin is to *know* Moscow.

Upon entering the Spassky Gate, or Gate of the Redeemer, every hat has to be removed in honour of the *ikon* of the Saviour which is placed above it. The picture was placed there, by the Tsar Alexis, in 1647, to be regarded as the "palladium of the Kremlin," and the order was given then that hats should be removed when passing through. The law is rigorously enforced still, and though it is sometimes a trial—I had frostbite in consequence when I last went through a year ago—yet the act is almost an instinctive one when entering or leaving the Kremlin.

Warsaw, again—for no one in this generation can dissociate it from Russia and call it Polish only—with its glorious position on the Vistula in the midst of its great plain, though not so ancient and inspiring as Cracow, in Galicia, is full of moving appeal to the national and historic sense for those who visit it for the first time, and especially, as in my own case, when entering the empire by that route. I have seen Warsaw in spring, summer, and winter, and always felt its charm; and I have not felt more deeply moved for a long time than by the Emperor's proclamation that he intended the Poles once more to be a nation and—there can be but little doubt about it—with Warsaw as its capital.

Riga also, the great shipping-port on the Baltic, which I have entered by sea and by land, and when coming in by sea have had the pleasure of seeing our beautiful English church on the shore with its graceful spire standing out conspicuously, yet blending in with other towers and pinnacles. How very characteristic of the Baltic and attractive the city is, with its blending of the Teuton and Slav populations! But how essentially Russian it is in all its leading features, while different from all other Russian cities! It is so wherever one goes both on this and on the other side of the Urals. There always seems to be something specially characteristic in these great centres of population; and they all seem as if, unlike other towns, they had each their own interesting story to tell for those who have ears to hear.

Town or city life in Russia is not very representative of the true life of the country and its people, though it undoubtedly exerts a widespread influence upon their general social life; for Russia's vast population is not gathered together in either towns or cities, but in hamlets and villages. Sir Donald Mackenzie Wallace tells us that when he wrote his first book on Russia, in 1877, there were only eleven towns with a population of over 50,000 in European Russia, and that, in 1905, they had only increased to thirty-four. The increase of the future will no doubt be more rapid when the war is over.

The great cities will probably, as practically all the cities of Europe have done of late years, follow the lead of Paris under Baron Hausmann in the character of their imposing blocks of houses and wide boulevards, and one capital will be much the same as any other in Europe in its general appearance and social life.

Russian cities, however, even the capital, though ever becoming more cosmopolitan, still possess their many distinctive and interesting features, costumes, and customs, and are most picturesque and interesting, of course, during the long winter. It gives one a shock almost to go for the first time to Warsaw or Petrograd—at Moscow there is always the Kremlin—in the middle of the summer. There is little to distinguish them then, apart from the ever-glorious beauty of the churches, from Buda-Pest or Vienna.

But in the winter! Then it is everywhere still characteristic Russia. The sledges, for instance, with their *troikas*! They are the same carriages or *droschkes* as in summer, but with runners instead of wheels. Horses are harnessed in the same way in both seasons, and even the coachmen seem to wear exactly the same dress all the year round, edged with fur like their caps, though the padding inside the coat *must* be less in summer, one would think. The sledges of nobles and other wealthy people, used in the winter only, are painted and decorated most attractively. To drive out on a winter night, under a sky brilliant with stars, the air extraordinarily keen, bracing, and stimulating, the bells tinkling from the high and graceful yoke which rises from the central horse of the three, wrapped in furs, and with no sounds but the bells and the crack of whips and the subdued crunching of the snow, is to taste one of the joys of life, and feel to the full, with happiness in the feeling, "This is Russia!"

A Well-clad Coachman.

The coachmen pad up their robes of blue to an enormous extent, so that they seem to bulge out over their seat. It is said to be a custom dating from Catherine's days and from her requirements that there should be at least twelve inches of good stuff between her coachman's skin and her nose! But the present reason for the custom, which prevails, as far as I know, in no other country, is that there is an objection to a thin coachman. When I was speaking of the absurdity of these grotesque padded-out figures to a lady whom I had taken into dinner one night in Moscow, she at once said:—

"Well, I must say I like my coachman to look comfortable and well fed, I should hate a thin one."

Dickens's fat boy in Pickwick must commend himself to Russia, for they love Dickens and read him in translation and the original all through the empire, as just what a driver ought to be. I should think coachmen in Russia, however, *ought* to be fat without any padding-up, for they are all merry and good-tempered, their blue eyes and pleasant faces under their furry caps giving the impression of perfect health. They sit on their boxes all day without any violent exercise, and probably have good and abundant food, and above all they sleep. However long you keep your coachman, even in the depth of winter, he does not mind, for he invariably seems to go to sleep while waiting, and to have an absolutely unlimited capacity for gentle and peaceful slumber. I am not at all sure whether my driver on the steppes has not usually been asleep even when we have been going at full speed, the centre horse trotting swiftly, the other two, according to custom, at the gallop.

The *dvornik* is another institution in town life. He is an indoor servant in great houses, usually about the front hall, to open the door for those who go out, ready for all sorts of odd things; or he may be a head out-of-doors servant; or he may give general help for three or four or more smaller establishments; but he has to be there, and cannot be dismissed, for he is *ex officio* a member of the police and has to make his report from time to time. It must give a little sense of espionage, but still, as with the passport, it is only the evil-minded or evil-living who need to be afraid of the *dvornik's* report, and it must be remembered also that the Russian Government has long had cause to dread the revolutionary spirit, and has had to fight for its very life against it.

This is the darker side of life in Russia; and as far as my experience goes it is the only dark side, for it must be evident that a designing *dvornik* may do untold harm, and specially—as I have known to be the case—in official and diplomatic establishments. The custom opens out possibilities of blackmail also, and one can only hope that it will pass away in what so many of us feel are to be for Russia the better days to come.

Russians are very hospitable, not only lavish in its exercise where ample means allow, but naturally and by custom thoroughly and truly ready, even in the homes of the very poor, to welcome the coming guest.

This is brought out in every book one reads of Russia, but by no one more touchingly than by Mr. Stephen Graham in his *Tramp's Sketches*, when he journeyed constantly amongst the very poor and found them always ready to "share their crusts." Sir Donald Mackenzie Wallace says the same about the wealthier classes: "Of all the foreign countries in which I have travelled Russia certainly bears off the palm in the matter of hospitality."

An interesting feature of a Russian meal, luncheon, or dinner, is its preliminary, the *zakouska*. It probably dates from the time when guests came from long distances, as they do still in the country, and would be hungry upon their arrival, and yet would have to wait until all the guests had come.

It would be, and indeed in some houses to which I have been is still, understood, that if you were asked for a certain time the dinner would follow in the course of an hour or two; and so the "snack" was provided, and laid out upon the sideboard. The great dinners or banquets in London are "7 for 7-30," to give time for guests to assemble.

The *zakouska*, however, remains the custom still at every meal, and consists of caviare sandwiches, *pâté de foie gras*, and various kinds of deliciously cured fish. Strangers to the country, not understanding this particular custom, for it is provided in the drawing-room, ante-room, or in the dining-room itself, sometimes enjoy it so much and partake so freely, that they feel unequal to the meal which follows, and then have the pain of seeing their host and hostess quite mortified and hurt by their not doing full justice to the good things provided. I remember being entertained at supper in Libau by the good consul and his family, at the St. Petersburg Hotel, when the *zakouska* provided was so abundant and attractive that we all decided that we could not go beyond it to anything more substantial.

Another special and characteristic feature of Russian life, and one which it seems impossible to transplant to another country, for many of my friends have tried it, is the *samovar* or large urn with a central flue for burning or smouldering charcoal. The *samovar* is always near at hand, and ready to be brought in at short notice to furnish what one can only call the national beverage of tea. The steaming urn is a very cheerful object in the room, and when tea is made and guests are served, the teapot is placed on the top of the central flue and everything is kept bubbling hot. On the steppes I used to boil my eggs in the space between the flue and the outside cover, though this was not held to be good for the tea. Tea is provided and enjoyed everywhere in Russia, drunk very hot, rather weak and almost always with sugar, though *not* with lemon except in great houses and hotels. "Slices of lemon," to my amazement I was told, as I travelled off the track of railways and sometimes on, "are an English custom!"

Tea is always taken in tumblers set in a little metal frame with a handle. On the trains for the poorest passengers there is often hot water, and always at stations on the way; and emigrants, as they travel, may be said to do so teapot in hand. It is China tea and light in colour, and, as the custom amongst the poorer classes is to put only a moderate quantity of tea into the *tchinak* or teapot, to begin with, and to fill up with hot water as they go on drinking for an indefinite time, it must be very weak indeed at the end. Not even at the start is it strong, or what some public schoolboys call "beefy." At the end it can hardly have even a flavour of tea about it, though they go on drinking it quite contentedly. Across the Urals and amongst the Kirghiz I found the custom was not to put sugar in the tea but in the mouth, and drink the tea through it, and just above the Persian frontier jam was taken in the same way, to flavour and sweeten the tea in the act of drinking.

Russian houses, in the great cities, are much the same as in other capitals, though perhaps rather more spacious and richly furnished. The rooms for entertainment and daily use open out of each other, of course, and the beautiful stoves of porcelain have not, as yet, given way to central heating. Double windows in all the rooms are the rule all through the long winter, with a small pane let in for ventilation; and thus a cosy and comfortable sense of warmth is experienced everywhere whilst indoors, which renders it, strange as it may seem, unnecessary to wear, as in our own country, warm winter under-garments. Comfortably warm by night or day, without extra clothing or extra blankets whilst indoors, and wrapped in thick warm furs when out of doors, the winter is not as trying in Russia as in more temperate countries. One takes a cold bath, indeed, in that country with more enjoyment than anywhere else, for, though the water gives an almost electric shock with its icy sting, yet, as soon as one steps out into the warm air of the bath-room and takes up the warm towels, the immediate reaction brings at once a glow of pure enjoyment. There is every comfort in a Russian house, especially in the winter.

The country house, or *datcha*, is a necessity for those who have to live in Russia all the year round, as the cities and great towns are very hot and dusty, and often full of mosquitoes in the two or three months of summer, which is quite tropical in its character.

Thus there are the two extremes, an Arctic winter and a tropical summer.

The country houses are entirely summer residences, with great verandahs and balconies and other facilities for life in the open, and are often placed amongst pine-woods or by the sea. Some of my friends use their *datchas* in winter also; and it is interesting to see how balconies and verandahs which in summer are filled with carpets, furniture, and plants, and are quite open on every side to meet the needs of the family and its guests all through the day in the open air, in winter are closed in by double windows fitted in on every side, and thus are made into additional and altogether different rooms.

The homes of the Russian nobility are very richly and artistically appointed in every particular. I stayed with friends a couple of years ago who had taken such an establishment for the summer; and furniture, pictures, china, arrangements and decorations of rooms all gave striking testimony to the wealth and cultivated tastes of the absent family. Even beyond the Urals, at the Kyshtim Mine, when first I visited it and was the guest of the managing director, I was amazed at the sumptuous character of his abode built by the former owners of the mine.

It is a vast building approached by a great courtyard and in the Greek style of architecture, with towers in different places giving it a fortress-like appearance in the distance. The rooms are extraordinarily large and numerous, and here and there are bits of Venetian furniture, old paintings, and rich carpets. On going straight through the great salon, which one enters from the outer door and into the open air on the other side, one is again under a great portico with Greek pillars, capitals, and frieze, looking out over a large sheet of water towards hills and forests. I could not help saying to myself in amazement the first time I went there, "And this is Siberia!"

I am not at all sure that social life upon European lines will not develop more rapidly in Siberia than in European Russia. Even now I do not know any railway station in Russia proper that can compare with that of Ekaterinburg, just where Siberia really begins, in all its arrangements for the travelling public and especially in the equipment of its restaurant and dining-rooms, where every comfort in the way of good food and good service is provided for the traveller, and French and German are freely spoken.

It is impossible to write on the general social life without mentioning, though one cannot do more, certain recent events which must have a tremendous influence upon Russia's future, socially as well as nationally. There is, for instance, the Emperor's proclamation against the *vodka* monopoly hitherto enjoyed by the government, which prohibits State *vodka* selling for ever. The effect upon the public life of the great cities has been astonishing already. No one could have believed that the "stroke of a pen," so to speak, could have wrought such a change in the habits of a people. It remains to be seen, of course, how long the change will last; but, though Acts of Parliament cannot make people sober, it is a grand step in the right direction to decide that they shall not make them drunk, as the encouragement given by the State to the sale of *vodka* must certainly have done.

Could any other modern government have made a sacrifice such as Russia has made in giving up the expectation of nearly £100,000,000 of revenue for the social well-being of her people? Truly she deals with "large spaces!"

Moreover, the *vodka* proclamation comes in the natural course of things, and can have been but very little hurried by the war; for things were already moving in that direction. Last year but one—1913—a scheme of "local option" was introduced into the empire; and, in every commune within its boundaries, I am assured, men and women alike having the vote for the purpose, the inhabitants were allowed to decide for themselves whether they would allow *vodka* to be sold in their villages and towns. It was recognized that if the men enjoyed getting drunk the wives and mothers were the sufferers, and so they were allowed to vote.

The whole country, therefore, before the war broke out, was prepared to face a great issue. And the general war cry, "We've a greater foe to fight than the Germans!" shows how they faced it, and gives them that ideal which should enable them to go far. They are out for a holy war, and far-reaching influences are clearly at work which will profoundly and permanently affect the whole social conditions and well-being of the people.

Then there is the proclamation concerning the resuscitation of Poland. This also does not come at all as an overwhelming surprise to many of us, as it has been fairly well known that the Emperor, and some at least of his principal advisers, have for some time had ever-increasing constitutional, even democratic, sympathies. It has been more and more felt of late that what is called Russification, as practised towards the Finns, would go no further; and indeed, as far as they were concerned, would be reversed. No thoughtful person who has marked the trend of events since 1908 could doubt the direction in which higher and responsible Russian thought was moving. But who can possibly foresee the far-reaching effect of raising up a great Polish nation once more and recognizing the Roman Catholic Church as the Church of that part of the empire, with Russians and Poles, Orthodox and Roman Catholic living together in amity and international unity?

"I have just been staying," writes Mr. Stephen Graham in the *Times* for October 29, 1914, "in the fine old city of Wilna, a city of courtly Poles, the home of many of the old noble families of Poland. It is now thronged with Russian officers and soldiers. Along the main street is an incessant procession of troops, and as you look down you see vistas of bayonet-spikes waving like reeds in a wind. As you lie in bed at night you listen to the tramp, tramp, tramp of soldiers. Or you look out of the window and see wagons and guns passing for twenty minutes on end, or you see prancing over the cobbles and the mud the Cossacks of the Don, of the Volga, of Seven Rivers. In the days of the revolutionary outburst the Poles bit their lips in hate at the sight of the Russian soldiers, they cursed under their breath, darted out with revolvers, shot, and aimed bombs. To-day they smile, tears run down their cheeks; they even cheer. Whoever would have thought to see the day when the Poles would cheer the Russian troops marching through the streets of their own cities? The Russians are forgiven!"

No one who has known Russia and Poland before the war could read this description without deep emotion.

"A very touching spectacle," he continues, "may be seen every day just now at the Sacred Gate of Wilna. Above the gateway is a chapel with wide-open doors showing a richly-gilded and flower-decked image of the Virgin. At one side stands a row of leaden organ-pipes, at the other stands a priest. Music is wafted through the air with incense and the sound of prayers. Down below in the narrow, muddy roadway kneel many poor men and women with prayer-books in their hands. They are Poles. But through the gateway come incessantly, all day and all night, Russian troops going to the front. And every soldier or officer as he comes lifts his hat and passes through the praying throng uncovered. This is beautiful. Let Russia always be so in the presence of the Mother of Poland."

It is impossible to read of that scene also, and recall at the same time past relations of the two Churches here mentioned, without dreaming dreams and seeing visions of social unity such as has never yet been known, both for Russia and all other countries to which she has so nobly and unselfishly given a social lead and invitation to follow on.

Note from p. 27, "M. Bourtzeff."—There was a notice in the *Times* of February 4th last as follows: "A Reuter telegram from Petrograd of yesterday's date states that M. Bourtzeff has been sentenced to deportation to Siberia." I have never been able, however, to obtain any confirmation of this from Russian officials in this country, nor do the Russian Embassy know anything about it. I hope it will prove that a sentence was passed *pro forma*, and that the Emperor, as in Miss Malecska's case, at once remitted the sentence, or that M. Bourtzeff was merely requested to live in Siberia for the present rather than in Russia, and I personally should think that no great hardship. I feel that we must await further particulars before being able to form correct impressions of this important case.

FOOTNOTES:

[1] See end of this chapter, p. 45.

CHAPTER III
THE PEASANTRY

It would be much more satisfactory to one's self to try and write a *book* about the peasantry of Russia, rather than attempt to say all that one wants to say in a single chapter, for there could hardly be any more interesting and promising people in the world than the peasant folk of Russia. The future of the empire depends upon the development and improvement of its agricultural population, as they form three-fourths, according to the last census of three years ago, of its grand total of over 171,000,000 souls. Russia thus leads in the white races in the matter of population, and possesses that splendid asset, which Goldsmith feels to be vital to a nation's advance and with which nothing else can compare when lost:—

"Princes and lords may flourish, or may fade;
A breath can make them as a breath has made;
But a bold peasantry, their country's pride,
When once destroyed can never be supplied."

It is upon coming to write even briefly and in an impressionist kind of way upon a class which forms the huge majority of Russia's population that the vastness of her empire and the different conditions under which her people live begin to be in some small degree apparent. It is no wonder that thoroughly well-informed and experienced writers, who have lived long and travelled far in the country and who are evidently quite to be trusted, should yet write so differently.

A Village Scene.

One will write as if the Russian peasant was only a degree better in his intelligence than the animals which share his filthy hovel, and no less brutish in temperament and nature. Fearsome pictures are drawn in some books I have read of the almost impossible conditions and indescribable filth in which men, women, and children, fowls, pigs, horses, cattle, and dogs herd together in a stifling atmosphere and sickening stench, where to enter is out of the question unless one is to be covered with vermin and contract some illness. All this may be true to the writer's own experiences, and he can only write and describe things as he has found them; but I too will do the same.

It is worth while to remember from the first that the lives of the peasant population of Russia must be as different in summer and winter as tropical heat is from arctic cold. In the winter all *must* crowd in together when the household is poor if life has to be preserved and defended against that appalling cold, when the one condition of the survival is warmth, or even heat. All outdoor occupation ceases, of course, with the one exception, it may be, of cutting, stacking, and carting wood. A peasant population, with a not very advanced civilization as yet, and little education—only twenty per cent. of the whole population can read and write—must, like the animal world, hibernate, come as it were to a standstill, rest physically and mentally, and prepare for the unremitting activities of the summer.

I remember once when staying in an inn at the top of an Alpine pass being impressed with the extraordinary energy and vivacity of the head waitress. She was simply untiring, always in good spirits, always at hand when wanted, unfailing in her attentions; however late a guest was up she was moving cheerfully about, however early one was down she was down before him helping to get things ready. When I was leaving I said to her, "I've been wondering when you get your rest?"

She smiled brightly, and said cheerfully, "In the winter, sir."

That's when the Russian peasant gets his rest also, and with the spring he begins his energetic life of farming and agriculture, of carting and labour. The long days are busy and all too short, the brief nights are hardly more than an interval. The whole land is full of movement, the air is full of song and music, the holidays marked by game and dance. Nothing could be more unlike the bitter cold and gloom of Russia's long and terrible winter than the glow, brilliance, joy, and never-ceasing activities of her amazingly rich and life-giving summer. Her peasantry must present the same contrasts in homes and seeming temperaments, and two writers may therefore be widely asunder in their descriptions, and yet both write truthfully of the things they have seen and known at different times of the year.

To me the Russian peasant is, as to others who have known him at his best, an amiable, attractive, intelligent, thoroughly good-natured and altogether lovable creature. It is quite true that he can do, has done, and may again do some perfectly appalling things, but it has been when thoroughly worked up, as one of a crowd, and when every one else has lost his head. Terrible things which were not allowed to be known in Europe outside their frontiers, and now will probably never be known, were done during the revolution of seven years ago. But the Russian peasants are like children, as yet, and any one who knows and loves children knows perfectly well also what they are capable of, if they have any spirit in them, when thoroughly worked up, and when they too have for the time being lost their head and feel capable of almost anything that will hurt and pain and annoy. The peasants are in this, as in many other things, like children.

As soon as the statistics of the Russian peasantry come to be examined a startling fact comes to light. More than half their number—582 out of every 1,000—die before they are five years old. This means, as in the more inclement parts of our own country, that those who survive are a hardy race, strong and virile. The mortality is greatest amongst male children—over 600 out of every 1,000—and those, therefore, who do live are strong enough for anything and of amazing vitality, as we have seen in the present war.

Not only are they vigorous and strong in physique, however, but there is nothing lacking in their intelligence, or Russia would not have the charm and fascination she possesses. Probably no country in the world, unless it be still agricultural France, can compare with Russia in the character of its peasant industries or their importance as part of the national revenue and resources. Probably the people will be stimulated to greater industry in this direction by the removal of the *vodka* temptation, and both cease to feel the desire for it and get something in its place. Just as a man I once knew who was led to give up drink and gambling at the same time, when wondering how he could possibly live without them, had to change his house and remove to another with a garden. There in gardening work he found his compensation, and at the same time added to the resources of his household. Thus may it be in Russia.[2]

The list of the Russian peasant industries is a long and interesting one, but I won't take up time in enumerating them, as they can be found in the *Russian Year Book*, or probably in most encyclopaedias. I may perhaps mention a few which have especially interested and attracted me, and will no doubt be brought before our own people in the Russian shops and exhibitions which are almost certain to be opened before long, and it must be remembered that I am speaking of peasant productions only.

There is the beautiful "drawn thread" work, lace-like in character, that all my friends say is unlike anything to be found in our own country, the making of which is promoted by the Princess Tenisheva and other Russian ladies, as well as embroidered and worked linen of all descriptions. Toys, and particularly large ornamental wooden spoons, of all kinds are made in great quantities by village folk, and painted boxes such as the Japanese make, but with Russian scenes upon them, in delightful shades of colour, and with rich and brilliant lacquer inside and out. Then there are hand-woven laces of different varieties, and, above all, the Orenburg shawls, exquisitely dainty and so fine that the largest of them will go through a wedding-ring, and yet warmer than Shetland wool. These also are hand-woven, and come from the province of Orenburg, just beyond the Urals.

Ironwork, again, is a speciality in Siberia, where they are said to be the best iron-workers in the world, though a friend of mine to whom I mentioned this, when I was showing him some perfectly wonderful and artistic specimens which had been given to me when I first went to Siberia, said, "That's because they have the best iron in the world." The stone or gem-cutting industry is an important one. Furs, from sheep and wolf-skins up to bears, as well as those of foxes, sables, elk, and reindeer, and other animals, are perfectly dressed by the peasants for their own use, as well as for sale. I have some exquisite work in coloured silks upon hand-woven cloth which had never been out of the tents where they were made till given to me, and above all I cherish a silver box which had been made in a Kirghese *uerta* or tent, far away upon the steppes, and was given to me when I had had services there after my long drive in the *tarantass*. It would hold about a hundred cigarettes, and was given to me for that purpose, is oblong in shape, with a lid of sloping sides, and is made from silver roubles hammered out and ornamented with that beautiful damascening that is said to be a lost art except for the peasants of the steppes. It is such a beautiful bit of workmanship that any one looking at it would think it had come out of a Bond Street silversmith's, until he turned it over and saw that the bottom is a plain piece of iron, rough and unornamented. Let no one think the Russian peasant unintelligent or unskilful or wanting in dexterity or resource. The wonder to me is that, with the few advantages and opportunities he has had, he is so capable, intelligent, and quick to learn as he is. And what is important for us to remember is that he loves to learn from an Englishman.

Then, again, we are told that he is brutish in temperament and of low ideals, and never seems to rise above his squalid surroundings. I don't agree that his surroundings *are* squalid. Simple they are, without a doubt, as the Canadian shack of three brothers I know is simple, and has nothing in it but beds and tables and chairs, their boxes and saddle-trees, etc., and all is bed and work, but it is not squalid. They have been brought up in a good and refined home, and yet find nothing incongruous in their present abode amongst the pine-woods.

That's what a Russian peasant's home is also, simple and yet attractive. It is built of logs, the interstices well plastered up with moss and clay to keep out all cold air, cool in summer and warm in winter by reason of the thickness of these outer walls; and it usually has an inner entrance or small room, before the large and chief living-room. There will be two or more small square windows in the latter, an *ikon* in a corner with a lamp before it and a shelf for flowers below—every one on entering looks towards it, bowing reverently and making the sign of the Cross—a very large stove of bricks, whitewashed, upon the top of which rests a wide shelf, carried along the wall as far as is necessary for the whole family to be able to find sleeping-space upon it. There will also be a long wooden bench, a great table, a few wooden stools, and a great cupboard, and, nearly always, cheap coloured pictures of the Emperor and Empress, whose portraits are to be found in all shops, inns, post offices, and places of public resort.

These are the simple surroundings described and made familiar to us by all writers of Russian stories of which peasants form a part, and all over the empire they are found just as Tolstoi, Dostoviesky, Turgenieff, and others bring them before us in their interesting tales. Take for example Tolstoi's *Where Love is there God is also*, *Master and Man*, and other parables and tales. When Martin Avdeitch is looking out from his small abode through his one small window upon the passers-by as simply as man could do, and yet with shrewd and discerning eyes, he is ready for the old pilgrim who comes into his life just at the right moment, and shows him the way to God.

Or take Nikita in *Master and Man*, in the same volume. In some ways he is extraordinarily simple, and does not appear to know how shamefully he is being exploited by his avaricious and grasping master. We are told in the story that he *does* know even though he goes on as if he didn't, and does his duty by him as if he were the best of masters, just as he does by an unfaithful and unfeeling wife. It would be difficult to imagine a peasant one would more love to know and understand than Nikita, strong, capable, affectionate, and shrewd, as he comes running before us in the story, to harness the horse for his master, the only man on the place that day not drunk, talking to the little brown cob which noses him affectionately, and in the end making a tremendous struggle for his own and his master's life, and winning through himself. Thus he goes on steadily as long as he lives, with no other thought but that of duty, until he lies down beneath the *ikon*, and, with the wax candle in his hand just as he had always wished, passes away at peace with every living creature and with GOD.

There are no peasants like the Russians, or who think as they do. They are young, one feels, and "The thoughts of youth are long, long thoughts," and that is just what those who know them best find out.

A friend of mine told this story the other day at a meeting, at which we both had to speak, and I am sure it will bear repetition. A *moujik*, or peasant, was driving a German commercial traveller across the open country, and in the course of their conversation together his companion said to him:—

"Your countrymen are nothing but a lot of idolaters. You worship those *ikons* of yours, and bow down to them as the heathen do," and so on. The *moujik* was very indignant, and grumbled out his disapproval of all this.

"Worship our *ikons* indeed! We don't." And as they went driving on he suddenly drew up, and, pointing to a tree, demanded of the astonished traveller:—

"Do you mean to say that I would worship that tree?"

"No, no. Of course not! Drive on."

With a very disapproving grunt he drove on, and when they reached their destination, where there was a painter at work upon an outside door, the *moujik*, pointing to the paint-pot beside it, again demanded of the traveller:—

"Would you say I could worship that paint?"

"No, certainly not! You could not be so silly."

"But yet you say I worship an *ikon*, which is only painted wood, and can't see that I only use it to help me to worship GOD."

Let the reader reflect upon the way in which that peasant had been thinking over the charge made against him of idolatry, thinking what idolatry really was, and how far he felt himself from it. Let him try and imagine how one of our own agricultural labourers would think over such a subject if he were entering into conversation with us as he was digging in our garden, or driving us in a farmer's cart to a country station. I am writing this chapter in a quiet part of the country, and I can't conceive of any of the labouring people here even approaching that line of thought upon which the mind of that *moujik* began at once to move, though slowly enough no doubt, when he was told he was little better than a worshipper of idols.

I read the other day in a book on Russia that the peasantry are very dirty in person, and never wash; but again it must be borne in mind, as another remarkably well-informed and sympathetic writer[3] says also: "When people generalize about the intense misery of Russian peasants and the squalor in which they live they should remember that Russia is a large country, that it possesses a North and a South, an East and a West, and that what is true about one place is quite untrue about another." I shall be quite prepared, therefore, to be told by people who know Russia far better than I can ever hope to do, that their experience has been altogether different from my own, and I shall not dream of questioning or doubting the truth of what they say as far as their own experience goes.

In this vast area of which we are thinking there must indeed be great varieties of experience and conditions of life, and it is not contrary to what one might expect to find much nearer home, that the people of one village may be clean in their habits and those of another quite the reverse. But from all I have seen, heard, and read the Russian labouring and peasant class have a great desire to be clean. Nor is this a new thing at all in the national life. It is nearly forty years ago since Sir Donald Mackenzie Wallace told us, in the first edition of his work, of the important part taken by the weekly vapour-bath in the life of the Russian peasantry, and described "the public bath possessed by many villages." How many villages of our own, even now, have a public bath? And how many of our own peasantry dream of having what is a perfectly ordinary and weekly habit of the Russians—the bath in his own house?

My Russian and Siberian friends tell me how they have always to arrange for their domestic servants to get a good bath, before they change for Sunday, every Saturday afternoon and evening. Mr. Rothay Reynolds says the same: "My friend took me to see his bath-house. Russians are exceedingly clean. In villages one may see a row of twenty cottages, and, thirty yards from them, a row of twenty bath-houses. The one the peasant showed me was a hut with a stove intended to heat the great stones placed above it. On bath nights the stove is lit, and when the stones are hot a bucket of water is thrown on them, so that the place is filled with steam. The bather lies on a bench in the suffocating atmosphere, soaps himself, and ends his ablutions with ice-cold water. In town and country it is held to be a religious duty to take a steam-bath once a week. Servants ask if they can go out for a couple of hours to visit one of the great baths in the cities. They go away with clean linen bound up in a handkerchief, and return shining with cleanliness. Admission to the cheapest part of a steam-bath is usually a penny farthing, but in the great towns there are luxurious establishments frequented by the rich."

There is another custom connected with the bath which testifies to the hardy character of the Russian *moujik*. They often rush straight out of the almost suffocatingly hot bath which they have been taking *inside* the huge earthenware oven that they all possess and, naked and steaming, roll themselves contentedly and luxuriously in the snow. This, as a writer has well said, "aptly illustrates a common Russian proverb which says that what is health to the Russian is death to the German"—a proverb which has had striking illustration again and again this very winter. Probably some of my readers saw the account of the arrival at the Russian front, soon after war began, of the bath-train which was so completely furnished and arranged that two thousand men could have a clean bath during the day or twelve thousand in the course of the week. No doubt others have followed since then.

The bath to the Russian has a certain religious significance also, as in Moslem countries; "and no good orthodox peasant," I have read, "would dare to enter a church after being soiled with certain kinds of pollution without cleansing himself physically and morally by means of the bath." "Cleanliness is next to godliness" is not a bad motto for any people, and possibly Russians will like to know that we have an order of knighthood which dates from 1398, and is named "The Most Honourable Order of the Bath," and mentioned regularly in the services at Westminster Abbey.

A great sense of initiative and personal responsibility, as well as corporate spirit at the same time, is clearly given early in life to the peasant mind in Russia, for nowhere, I fancy, in the world, except in countries where primitive ideas and customs still obtain, is there the same standard of village life and self-government. There are two kinds of communities. First, there is the village community with its Assembly or *Mir*, under the presidency of the *Staroshta*, who is elected by the village. He presides over the Assembly, which regulates the whole life of the village, distributes the land of the commune, decides how and when the working of the land has to be done; and it is specially interesting to know that in this most remarkable and exceptional village government of the *Mir* all women who permanently and temporarily are heads of houses are expected to attend its meetings and to vote—no one ever dreams of questioning their right to do so.

In addition to the village assembly and chief elder there is also the "Cantonal" Assembly, consisting of several village communities together, meeting also under the presidency of a chief elder. All this is, of course, a development of family life where exactly the same ideas of corporate duty in its members, and responsibilities in its head, are held.

It is evident that Russia has a great future if this view of self-government is gradually carried upwards. The right beginning in constitutional government, surely, is in the family, for there we find the social unit. A state is not a collection or aggregate of individuals, but of families, and all history shows us that the greatness or insignificance of a country has always been determined by the condition of its homes and the character of its family life. If from the family, village, and commune Russian constitutionalists work slowly and carefully upwards, giving freedom to make opinions and convictions felt in the votes, just as responsibility is understood and met in the home, until one comes to the head of it all in "The Little Father"; and if he really rules—or administers rather, for no true father rules only—just as any good father would do, Russia the autocratic and despotic, associated in the minds of so many with arbitrary law in the interests of a few, enforced by the knout and prison-chain, may yet give the world a high standard of what the government of a free and self-respecting people ought to be.

I should doubt if any peasantry in the world live so simply and frugally or, as they say in the North of England, "thrive so well on it," as the Russians. The men are of huge stature, and their wives are strong, comely, and wholesome-looking also. Their boys and girls are sturdy, vigorous, and full of life; and yet how bare the table looks at the daily meal, how frugal the fare and small the quantity! It has been the greatest joy to me to have Russian boys and girls, in out-of-the-way places, to share my sandwiches or tongue or other tinned meats, when stopping at a rest-house, and see their eyes shine at the unexpected and unusual treat.

Black rye-bread and cabbage-soup form the staple food of a peasant family, while meat of any kind is rarely seen. The many and rigorous fasts of the Church make very little difference to the quality of the food, but only to its quantity. The thanks given by guests to their host and hostess, *Spasibo za kleb za sol*, "Thanks for bread and salt," tell their own story of a bare and simple diet. Many of us have read in *The Russian Pilgrims to Jerusalem* of the sacks of black and hard crusts the peasants take with them, which quite content them.

What a tremendous difference it must have made this winter in the Russian food transport from the base to the front, to know that, if a serious breakdown took place, or a hurried march was ordered with which it was difficult for them to keep up, and the worst came to the worst, the men would have their crusts. It has been said in years gone by, and may be true still in many places, that the Russian peasant's ideas of Paradise is a life in which he would have enough black bread to eat.

This bare subsistence and monotonous diet, perhaps, is responsible for the break-out from time to time when the attraction of *vodka* is too strong to be resisted in a life in which there are no counter-attractions. Counter-attractions there ought to be for a being who is created not for work alone, but for that recreation which, as its very name betokens, his whole nature needs if he is to do his best work. "There is a time to work and a time to play," says the proverb writer; and if we hold that in school life "All work and no play makes Jack a dull boy," we can hardly wonder that, the world over, those for whom work is provided and play refused will seek, as they have ever done, to make up for its absence by the exhilaration of stimulating and intoxicating drinks. It is when writing upon the drunkenness to be seen at every Russian village holiday that one whom I have often quoted in this book,[4] truly says, "As a whole a village fête in Russia is a saddening spectacle. It affords a new proof—where, alas! no proof was required—that we northern nations who know so well how to work have not yet learnt the art of amusing ourselves."

As an instance of the real and natural friendliness and essential good nature of the Russian, I may say that even when drunk I have never seen or heard of men quarrelling. They do not gradually begin to dispute and recriminate and come to blows or draw the knife, as some of the more hot-blooded people of the South do, when wine excites or spirits cheer them. They seem to become more and more affectionate until they begin to kiss each other, and may be seen thus embracing and rolling over and over together like terriers in the snow. If wine unlooses the tongue, and brings out what is usually hidden away beneath the surface, it evidently brings out nothing very evil from the inner life of the Russian peasant.

In time to come, if all's well, Russia is to be opened up to the traveller, and everywhere the British tourists will be welcomed, and even though the beaten track of the railway may never be left there will be abundant opportunities for observing the habits and customs of the people. A modern writer who, apparently, in passing through Siberia never went far from the railway, though he probably stayed for some time at different places on the way, and sat in third and fourth-class carriages even if he did not actually travel in them, managed to see a great deal of peasant life. The railway train is open from end to end, and a great deal may be learnt thus about the people while merely passing through. There are also the long waits at the stations where there are invariably interesting groups of the most romantic and picturesque character—the women vivacious and full of conversation, while the men stand more stolidly by, always making one long to speak and understand their language and to know more about them.

There is a story of Mr. Maurice Baring's which illustrates what I have already said of the way in which the Russian peasant mind begins to move freely, independently, and responsibly upon lines undreamed of by those who may be addressing him, and shows how far he is from receiving merely conventional and stereotyped impressions, but is always ready to think for himself. Mr. Baring considers it an instance of his common sense. The reader may also have his own ideas of what it illustrates, but the story is this:—

"A Socialist arrived in a village to convert the inhabitants to Socialism. He wanted to prove that all men were equal, and that the government authorities had no right to their authority. Consequently he thought he would begin by disproving the existence of GOD, because if he proved that there was no GOD it would naturally follow that there should be no Emperor and no policemen. So he took a holy *ikon* and said, 'There is no GOD, and I will prove it immediately. I will spit upon this *ikon* and break it to bits, and if there is a GOD He will send fire from heaven and kill me, and if there is no GOD nothing will happen to me at all.' Then he took the *ikon* and spat upon it and broke it to bits, and said to the peasants, 'You see GOD has not killed me.' 'No,' said the peasants, 'GOD has not killed you, but we will'; and they killed him.''

It is not difficult to imagine that closing scene, knowing Russia. There would be no excitement, but all would be quickly and effectually done.

The same writer draws our attention to Turgenieff's wonderfully appealing sketches of country life, though not many of his works have been translated for English readers as yet. He alludes especially in an essay of last year on "The Fascination of Russia" to his description of the summer night, when on the plain the children tell each other bogey stories; or the description of that July evening, when out of the twilight from a long way off a voice is heard calling, "Antropk-a-a-a!" and Antropka answers, "Wha-a-a-at?" and far away out of the immensity comes the answering voice, "Come home, because daddy wants to whip you!"

Perhaps the reader may *feel* nothing as he reads, but all who know and love Russia, and are stirred by thoughts of its life and people will feel that it was abundantly worth while to write down such a simple incident. They will understand and feel that stirring within, which Russia never fails to achieve again and again for those who have once lived and moved amongst her peasantry, and come under her strange spell and felt her charm.

Gogol, the greatest of Russian humorists, has a passage in one of his books, where, in exile, he cries out to his country to reveal the secret of her fascination:—

"'What is the mysterious and inscrutable power which lies hidden in you?'" he exclaims. "'Why does your aching and melancholy song echo unceasingly in one's ears? Russia, what do you want of me? What is there between you and me?' This question has often been repeated not only by Russians in exile, but by others who have merely lived in Russia.

"There are none of those spots where nature, art, time, and history have combined to catch the heart with a charm in which beauty, association, and even decay are indistinguishably mingled; where art has added the picturesque to the beauty of nature; and where time has made magic the handiwork of art; and where history has peopled the spot with countless phantoms, and cast over everything the strangeness and glamour of her spell.

"Such places you will find in France and in England, all over Italy, in Spain and in Greece, but not in Russia.

"A country of long winters and fierce summers, of rolling plains, uninterrupted by mountains and unvariegated by valleys.

"And yet the charm is there. It is a fact which is felt by quantities of people of different nationalities and races; and it is difficult if you live in Russia to escape it; and once you have felt it you will never be free from it. The aching melancholy song which, Gogol says, wanders from sea to sea throughout the length and breadth of the land, will for ever echo in your heart and haunt the recesses of your memory."[5]

The Metropolitan of Moscow.

FOOTNOTES:

[2] Just as I go to press Mr. Lloyd George has told the House of Commons that productivity is already increased 30 per cent. in Russia.

[3] The Hon. Maurice Baring.

[4] Wallace, *Russia*, vol. i, p. 129.

[5] *Russian Review* for February, 1914.

CHAPTER IV
THE CLERGY

The Russian Church is a daughter of the Byzantine Church—the youngest daughter—and only dates from the close of the tenth century, when monks came to Kieff from Constantinople during the reign of Vladimir. There would be little "preaching of the Cross of CHRIST," I should fancy, as the great means of conversion for that great mass of servile population. We are told, indeed, that Vladimir gave the word and they were baptized by hundreds at a time in the River Dnieper, and that no opposition was offered to the new religion as the old Nature worship had only very lightly held them, and had no definite priesthood.

The new religion, however, soon acquired a very strong hold upon the people of all classes, and the power and influence of the Church grew just as the State gained ever-new importance; the power of the Patriarch increasing as that of the Tsar increased, until in a comparatively short time the Orthodox Church stood alone, and owned no Eastern supremacy on the one hand, nor yielded to the approaches of the Roman Papacy on the other. By the end of the sixteenth century the other Eastern Patriarchs recognized and accepted the Patriarchate of Moscow as being an independent one, and fifth of the Patriarchates of the East.

This absolute independence only lasted about a hundred years, and the masterful Peter the Great laid his hands upon the Church as upon other parts of the national life, for he certainly had little cause to love the clergy, and appointed no successor to the Patriarch of Moscow when he died in 1700. It was very interesting to hear, from the Procurator of the Holy Synod himself, M. Sabloff, when I first went to Petrograd, what great importance Peter attached to this office when he constituted the Holy Synod in 1721 to take the place of the Patriarchate.

"He used to say," he mused, looking down upon the ground, "that the Procurator of the Holy Synod was the *oculus imperatoris* (the Emperor's right hand, literally 'the Emperor's eye')," and as he said so one could not but remember how his predecessor, M. Pobonodonietzeff had upheld that tradition, and, next to the Emperor, had himself been the most prominent and autocratic figure in the whole empire.

The Procurator, however, is not the President of the Holy Synod, as the Metropolitan of Petrograd fills that office, but he is present as the Emperor's representative, and though all the other members of the Synod are the highest ecclesiastical dignitaries of the Russian Church, yet as they are summoned by the Emperor, and his special lay representative is there always to represent and state his opinion and wishes, the Emperor himself must have an infinitely greater influence than our own sovereigns possess, though theoretically they fill the same office of "Defender of the Faith." He is described in one of the fundamental laws as "the supreme defender and preserver of the dogmas of the dominant faith," while immediately afterwards it is added "the autocratic power acts in the ecclesiastical administration of the most Holy Governing Synod created by it." The Emperor must have unlimited power, typified by his crowning himself at his coronation, in ecclesiastical administration, and the bishops and other clergy, who are intensely loyal, would probably not wish it otherwise; but he could not affect or change, even by a hair's breadth, any of the doctrines of the Church nor one of the ceremonies of its Liturgy.

Should the reader wish to know more about Church and State in Russia he will find a most admirable chapter (XIX) with that heading in Sir Donald M. Wallace's book. Interesting and important as the position of the Russian Church—in many ways so like our own—is for us to-day, it is only possible now to glance briefly at its constitution.

The clergy are divided into two classes, the black and the white, the black being the monastic and the white the secular and married clergy. All the patriarchs or archbishops, bishops, abbots, and higher dignitaries are taken from the ranks of the celibate and monastic clergy and have attained a high standard of education. All the parochial clergy, on the other hand, are educated in seminaries, or training colleges, but only those who show special ability go on to the academy, an institution which occupies the same position for the clergy as the university fills in civil education. They do not reach a very high standard as a rule, and before being appointed to a parish must be married. No unmarried priest can be in charge of a parish, and should he become a widower he must resign his parish, and either enter a monastery or retire into private life; but, in either case, he must not marry again.

Many years ago (1890) there appeared an interesting story of Russian life in the chief Russian literary magazine, and it was translated for the "Pseudonym Library" in a cheap form under the title of *A Russian Priest*.[6] It is still to be obtained, and it is most refreshing to read again this brief story of a brilliant young seminarist going on to the academy and attaining such distinctions, that he might have aspired to any high office in the Church, yet impelled by his ideals, and full of the CHRIST-like spirit, choosing the lowest grade of humble and village life, and "touching bottom," so as to speak, in his Church's work. As far as I can judge it describes still quite faithfully and clearly the relations of clergy and people in Russian villages and hamlets.

Let me now, however, speak briefly of some of the clergy I have met, taking such as I consider fairly representative of the different classes. I have felt myself that I have learnt a great deal more about the spirit and aims of the

Russian Church, and what we may regard as its present and future attitude to ourselves, from knowing its clergy and devout laity than ever I could have hoped to do by reading books about them, or from lectures, addresses, or letters written by them.

I will speak first of the Archbishop of Warsaw, who received me at Petrograd on my first visit, in place of the Metropolitan Antonius who had sent a very brotherly message of welcome from his sick-room, where shortly afterwards he died. The Archbishop Nicolai—Russians speak of their bishops and archbishops in this way, using the Christian name and not that of the See— is a most imposing and fatherly figure, and received me attired, just as his portrait shows him, wearing a very rich-looking satin robe, decorated with orders, and with a large cross of magnificent diamonds in the centre of his black cap or mitre. He had been in the United States, in charge of the Russian work there, and also in England, and spoke a little English, but it was so little that I was glad to have Mr. Feild, a churchwarden of the English Church, who has lived in Russia all his life, to be my interpreter.

His Grace was full of interest, sympathetic and intelligent, in all that I could tell him about our own Church at home, in Russia, and on the Continent generally, very keen to know of my impressions, and of my reception by the Procurator of the Holy Synod, and by the official at the Ministry of the Interior, who is responsible for religious administration. I shall have to speak later of the status of our Anglican Church in Russia, and so here I will only say that it led me to speak of the work of our Anglican Chaplain (the Rev. H. C. Zimmerman) at Warsaw, whereupon the archbishop said at once, "Ask him to come and see me when I am at Warsaw three months from now." I did so, and Mr. Zimmerman wrote to tell me afterwards that he had had the kindest reception, with quite a long conversation, had been presented with souvenirs, and dismissed with a blessing, his Grace saying to him as he left:—

"Now, regard me as your bishop, when your own is not here, and come to me whenever you are in need of advice or information."

The archbishop loves to think of his pleasant recollections of England and its Church life.

"Ah," he said, "your English Sunday! How beautiful it is to walk along Piccadilly on Sunday morning, with all the shops closed, and no one in the streets except quiet-looking people, all on their way to Church!"

London *is* very different in that respect on Sunday mornings, whatever it is later in the day, from every capital in the world. All is quiet, and Church and worship are in the air. Then the archbishop told me of his going to S. Paul's Cathedral, sitting in the congregation, and enjoying it all, until it had gradually come home to him during the Second Lesson that something was being read from one of the Gospels. On finding by inquiry that this was so, he rose at once to his feet, and looked with amazement upon the people *sitting* all round him while the Holy Gospel was being read. I'm afraid my telling him that we always stand for it in the Liturgy only added to his surprise, for he murmured to himself in a puzzled way, "Why in one place and not in another?"

Dear old man, he presented me with his portrait, here given, and all his published works, and hoped, as I do, that it would not be long before I went to see him again.

When at length the Metropolitan Antonius, after a long illness, passed away, he was succeeded by the Archbishop of Moscow who, in his turn, was succeeded by Archbishop Macarius, and it is of the last-named that I will next give briefly my experience. It was on January 10, 1914, according to our calendar, and on December 28, 1913, according to the Russian, when I had the feeling of being in two years at the same time, and of spending the same Christmas first in London and then in Russia, that he received me in his palace at Moscow. Palace it certainly is in the character and spaciousness of its rooms, but the furniture is what we should consider, in our own country, simple and rather conventional. The salon, or drawing-room, was very large, with the usual polished floor and rugs laid upon it. At one side two rows of chairs, facing each other, stood out from the wall, against which a sofa was placed, and in front of that a table. It was exactly the same at the Archiepiscopal Palace at Riga, where I had been a few months before, and the same procedure was followed on both occasions.

The Convent at Ekaterinburg, Siberia.

First the archbishop warmly embraced me, kissing me on either cheek and then upon the lips, and then courteously waved me to the seat of honour upon the sofa. At Riga when the archbishop took his seat upon the sofa he indicated the place beside him which I did not notice, and took the chair. But just as I was about to sit down, Madame Alexaieff, who had most kindly come to interpret, said hurriedly and in rather a shocked tone, "Take the seat beside him, he wishes it," and, remembering the etiquette of the sofa as observed still by old-fashioned people in Germany, I did as I was told.

At Moscow, however, I was more observant, and when the archbishop courteously waved his hand to the sofa I bowed to him and at once sat down, but only to find that he himself took a chair next me and left me alone in the place of dignity. It was quite in keeping with his whole bearing and conversation throughout, for he is evidently one of the most humble and unassuming of men. Yet he has covered himself with distinction in the course of his long life spent chiefly far away in the Altai country in Siberia, below Omsk, engaged in work of a missionary character. No one is more respected in the whole of Russia. He is just as shown in the portrait he gave me, slight and not tall, and his whole face lights up with keen interest as he talks and enforces his words with appropriate gestures. He was very caustic upon the subject of the non-attendance at church of educated and wealthy people in a certain place, which perhaps it will be kinder not to mention.

"No," he said, "they are never to be seen at any service, however important and solemn it may be. There are none there but the same common people who are always crowding into their churches. At least," he added more deliberately, "if the others are there, they adopt the common people's dress for the occasion!"

His expression and gesture as he said this were inimitable and indescribable, and the little touch of humour made one's heart warm towards him. He was much interested in hearing anything I could tell him of our own Church, and delighted, in a wistful sort of way, to hear the many details I gave him of its progress, especially in the extension of its missionary activities and ever-deepening interest in social questions and economic problems, as they affect the labouring classes and the very poor. His eyes sparkled as he too spoke of the poor, and told me what I should hear from the Grand Duchess Elizabeth, whom I was to see that afternoon, about the work to which she has given her life since the assassination of her husband, the Grand Duke Serge.

Like all his brethren of the episcopate he was greatly interested in anything I could tell him of the Archbishop of Canterbury and of his views and hopes about our own and the Russian Churches, and the Christian Church as a whole. He looked thoughtfully down as I spoke to him about unity and inter-communion under special circumstances, and said rather sadly:—

"How one would love more unity! But how much ground there is to be covered, how many difficulties to be cleared away before that can come!"

I smiled a little, at which he looked at me questioningly, and so I said:—

"I smiled because I thought of the brotherly and loving way in which you have received me to-day, and in which you are speaking so much and so freely of what is in your heart, and if these kind and friendly relations go on increasing between our Churches it will be progress such as He must love to see Who said 'By this shall all men know that ye are My disciples if ye have love one to another.' That will be progress of the best kind, and, even if it is slow, I for one shall greatly rejoice that we are moving at all in the right direction. Let us only keep moving, and we shall arrive in time."

We talked on about my own experiences the year before just to the south of where he had lived so long, and when I told him that I hoped this year to go to the Altai, his own actual country, he looked as though he envied me the journey. After embracing me again he accompanied me into the ante-room, where a poor peasant woman was waiting to see him with an *ikon* to be blessed. There was a great pile of quite cheap *ikons* for the poor, towards which he waved his hand and said, "And I have all these to bless also."

As I left I could only murmur to myself, "The dear old saint." He made me feel some sense of being back at Troas or Miletum or Ephesus, or coming out from the presence of Barnabas or Silas or St. Paul. It was truly apostolic!

Of course the interpreter makes a tremendous difference, but again, as at Petrograd and Riga, I had an excellent friend and helper in Mr. Birse, one of the churchwardens of our church in Moscow, who had spoken Russian all his life. I may add also that, as in Mr. Feild's case at Petrograd, he enjoyed the interview as much as I did, and would probably catch little subtleties of expression and self-revelation that would be lost to me by the hurried kind of interpretation that was necessary.

The next great dignitary I will try and describe, though I know I cannot possibly do justice to the dignity and nobility of character evident in all she says and does, is the Abbess Magdalena of the great Convent at Ekaterinburg in Siberia. The Convent is a most imposing group of buildings, stretching along an extended front, with cupolas, spires, and pinnacles, and is much frequented by pilgrims from far and near who come to pray in its chapel before a famous *ikon*. The Abbess and all her nuns wear the same kind of black dress, with cap and veil, quite black and unredeemed by any trace of white linen or cambric. The first thing that impressed me, even before I entered the gate, was the beauty of their singing. The choir were practising for a service on the Emperor's name-day on the morrow, and their hymn was the most beautiful thing I had ever heard from women's voices. It seemed to me that all the four parts were there. The bass certainly was, and I was told that the nuns with deep voices submitted them to careful training until they were able to reach very low notes indeed. There was, of course, no accompanying music, the conductor just waving her open hand to and fro to beat time, and the precision and crispness of the whole hymn were wonderful.

The chapel is a fine building beautifully painted by the nuns themselves, and its services are conducted by a priest and deacon. The deacon is a special feature in the ranks of the Russian clergy, and is responsible for all the choral parts of the services, apart from the actual priest's part in the Liturgy of course, and is chosen for the beauty of his voice. If a young man has a very fine voice and is wondering what use he shall make of it, he sees nothing at all unbecoming or incongruous in saying that he has not made up his mind yet whether he shall choose the Church or the stage.

The Abbess Magdalena.

When I was being introduced to the Ekaterinburg deacon, my friend and interpreter whispered to me, "He gave up the opera to come here." I thought, in my ignorance, that he had left the world for religion, and full of sympathetic interest said:—

"Ask him if he has ever regretted it!" and was rather disconcerted when he said in an off-hand way:—

"Oh! well of course I missed things at first, but I'm gradually getting used to it."

The Abbess confided to us that sometimes from the way he offered the incense she thought he must be thinking he was on the stage still.

He was a remarkably good-looking man with a wonderfully rich voice, and as none of the clergy ever cut hair or beard after Ordination, and his was just getting full, he looked a most picturesque and interesting figure. I should like to meet him again, and put the same question, in the hope of a somewhat more encouraging answer.

The Abbess, as well as managing and inspiring her sisters, superintends a really remarkable work. Her revenue is a very large one, and she gives a portion of it to the Bishop of Ekaterinburg for the work of his diocese—he is a young and energetic prelate whom I greatly liked when I knew him later—and out of the remainder she supports an Orphanage for six hundred girls in the Convent. The remarkable thing, however, about her management is its essentially practical, sensible, and considerate character. The girls do not wear a uniform, but can consult and improve their own taste in dress. They are carefully studied individually, and, while all are educated in school in the same way, special preparation is given for different callings in life according to the inclination and aptitude shown by the girls. Many, of course, prefer domestic service as being simpler and perhaps more in keeping with what they have known before coming there; but the more enterprising and competent can be, and are, taught all sorts of things which these very modern nuns do with such great ability themselves. They play, sing, do all sorts of "white work" for Russian and French purchasers, and are well up in modern photography. They carve, paint, make *ikons*, illuminate pictures, and do wonderful embroidery. There is a wide choice, therefore, for the girls under their charge, and they avail themselves of it to the full. Just before I was there a girl with a wonderful voice, after having been trained, had been launched, at the age of twenty-six, upon her career as a member of the Russian Imperial Opera.

I described this very modern work as carried out by the nuns of a very ancient convent, on my return, to the Archbishop of Canterbury, who remarked significantly, as I daresay many of my readers will, "And *that* is in Siberia!"

From Abbess let me pass to Abbot, but to a very different community. At Tiumen, the farthest point I reached in North Siberia, and where I had been to give services to a family living alone there, and from Scotland originally, I went out in the afternoon to see an old church outside the town where there had formerly been a fairly large monastery. It is very small and humble now, I am sure, from the few we saw there, and their neglected appearance as they went about their work in old and well-worn habits. The church was locked, but one of their number fetched the keys and showed us over the church, explaining their oldest *ikons*. As we walked towards the gate and our little carriage, he was full of curiosity about ourselves and our Church, and at last, as he questioned me rather closely, my friend could keep it in no longer, and explained:—

"He's a bishop, an English bishop, and he has come from London to give us lonely folk a service!"

The effect was extraordinary.

"An English bishop! Do you say it? Only to think of it! And I in my dirty clothes like any common labourer! And I am the Abbot! I beg of you! Oh! yes, I must insist. Do not deny me. Enter my humble house, and let me feel, even if you only take a seat upon a chair for a moment, that I have entertained you!"

Such hospitable intent was not to be withstood, and willingly enough we went with him into his small and, as he said, very humble abode, feeling how very touching and appealing it all was. We entered, our host saying cheerfully, "Be good enough to walk on," and found ourselves in a very bare and cheerless-looking parlour with stiff chairs, with black horsehair seats, round the walls, and a bare table in the centre, upon which stood a conventional and faded little basket of wax-flowers and fruit under a glass shade. On looking round we saw the good Abbot had disappeared, so we sat down and looked about us, hoping he had not gone off to order food; but in an incredibly short time, as if he had been a "lightning-change artist," he was back again. And what a transformation! The dirty and faded brown cassock was gone, and a flowing rich black robe had taken its place, a black mitre with dependent veil was upon his head, a magnificent chain and cross hung from his neck, and, thoroughly satisfied with his change, he looked as though he were saying "Now we meet upon equal terms!" His boyish delight was good to see as he said:—

"Now let me welcome you and greet you!" and he kissed me as other bishops had done.

These embraces are no light ordeal, as the good clergy never shave or cut their hair, and are very heavily bearded. But what of that, if one can feel as I did that day, when driving off and waving our adieux, that one had been breathing apostolic air, and had been very near in the spirit to "Peter and John"?

It only remains to give my experience of a typical parish priest, and then I shall feel that the Russian clergy have been fairly described.

Upon my arrival at the Spassky Mine, during my first journey in Siberia, in the very heart of the Kirghese Steppes, the manager told me what had passed between himself and the parish priest, kept there by his company to minister to the labourers in the smelting works. These were all Russians, though the labourers in the mine itself were chiefly Kirghese and Mohammedans.

"You will be interested to hear that our bishop is coming to see us," he had said by way of beginning.

"Your bishop! Where from and what for?"

"He is coming across the steppes, and from London, to give us services."

"You don't mean to say so!" was the startled exclamation. "I never heard of such a thing! Your bishop, all the way from London, driving night and day for five days across the steppes, to give you twenty English folk your services! Why, our bishop is only two or three days down the river at Omsk, but we could not expect him to come here for us."

"Well, you see," observed my friend, "our English Church does not forget her children, even if they are scattered far and wide. And we shall be glad to see him and receive Holy Communion and have sermons from him about our faith and highest duties."

After a moment's silence the priest looked up suddenly and said:—

"I wonder if your bishop will come to our service on Sunday and join with us in worship? If he will address us how glad we shall be to hear him!"

"He will certainly come, and, what is more, we will all come with him, and we will all be at divine service together for once. Suppose we have our Celebration at 7.30, and you arrange yours for 8.30 instead of 8.15, and we will all come over together? We shall fill our little room, and can't invite others; but we will all accompany the bishop to the church."

The Russian Priest at Spassky.

Next day (Sunday), after our Communion—all the staff received it—we went over, I in my robes, to the church, and were received by the wardens, the choir leading off with a hymn as we entered. The wardens at once conducted me behind the screen where the priest stood before the altar in his vestments, with a boy server on either side beautifully vested, the one in gold and the other in silver tissue.

After bowing to me gravely and reverently, he began the service. Nothing is *seen* of it by the congregation, and they hear only the voice of the priest, and are told from the other side of the screen what is passing within. The Russian Liturgy is full of traditional ceremonies, and rather bewildering, I should think, to an English Churchman; but there is no question as to the great reverence which distinguishes it. The priest confided to his manager afterwards how nervous he felt at celebrating with a bishop at his side, and how anxious he felt to make no mistake. He did not show it, however, and was as reverent and absorbed as any priest ought to be when back again in thought and word and deed in the Upper Room, where, on the same night on which He was betrayed, our LORD left us the memorial of His Passion and the Sacrament of His love and grace.

It was touching also to see the little servers struggling between curiosity and the claims of the service, but the latter triumphed; and not till they had taken off their little vestments and stood forth in their ordinary clothes did they permit themselves a good look at their strange visitor, and show themselves ready to have a word or two from him.

The priest, when he had taken an extra little service which some old men had asked for, came over to the manager's house and told me of his work, asked questions, and received little gifts, and told me how inspiring it was to all the Russians to know that their English staff were religious, as well as clever and able men, and glad to have their services when they could.

In one way this priest was not typical, for he was paid his stipend by the company, and not dependent upon his people. In all ordinary parishes this is not the case. The parish priest receives a nominal stipend from public sources, but depends upon his people for the rest. They give small contributions on their name days—a very substantial sum is received on S. John's Day, as a favourite Russian name is Ivan, or John—when the priest comes to bless their house or workshop, or for a marriage, christening, or funeral, or to give the Sacrament in illness. There is often, usually, indeed, bargaining on all these occasions. A portion of their fruits and crops is claimed. All sorts of contributions are made throughout the year, and, except in town parishes where able clergy have large incomes, given ungrudgingly by their people, the priest and his wife are always trying to get as much as they can for their services, and the people, who are very poor, to give as little.

This cannot lead to good relations between clergy and people, and, as the clergy in the country seldom if ever preach, there is no personal teaching to bring them together. Officially, therefore, it is true to say that the Russians value and reverence the ministry of their parish clergy, while, personally, they do not feel any great interest in them or their families, nor see any reason why they should. And certainly, as a rule—the fault of the system no doubt— they do not love them.

Let me now describe the service which I have mentioned upon a previous page, conducted after the Liturgy was over and the people had been dismissed. The priest told me four old men had asked to have a few special prayers and a reading from the Gospels, and I stayed to share it. The prayers were said, petition and response, by all five standing before the screen, after which the four old men, with rough and rugged faces, shaggy hair, and wide flowing beards, closed up together, and, as they stood back to back, the priest placed the beautifully-bound copy of the Gospels upon their heads and began to read. The rough faces seemed at once to change their whole expression: their blue eyes sparkled, and there appeared that light upon every countenance which "never was on sea or land," or anywhere else except upon the face of one who is in communion with God. My thoughts went back to the story of Moses as he came down from Sinai, and veiled his face as he spoke to the people, lest they should find there that which they could neither bear to see or understand. One's thoughts are always going back to scriptural scenes and descriptions when amongst the Russian peasantry.

S. Isaac's Cathedral, Petrograd.

FOOTNOTES:

[6] Published by T. Fisher Unwin, Paternoster Square.

CHAPTER V
RELIGIOUS LIFE AND WORSHIP

It is well sometimes to define our terms and phrases, and it is absolutely necessary in this case. What is it that we mean when we speak of the religious life of a people, Christian and non-Christian alike? Our soldiers have been fighting shoulder to shoulder with Hindoos and Mohammedans, whose British commander, on the eve of their first battle, addressed them in words which ought to be long remembered by those who are working and praying for the hastening of GOD's kingdom, appealing to their faith, and reminding them that prayers were ascending from Mosque and from Temple to the GOD of all, on their behalf.

The Hindoos and Moslems have their religious life as well as ourselves. And it behoves us of the Christian Church, especially when such stirring words can be addressed to two Eastern peoples, so widely different in their creeds, to remind them that their prayers are going up to the same "GOD of all," to look very earnestly and sympathetically at the religious life and worship of all the different Churches which make up the "Mystical Body of CHRIST and the blessed company of all faithful people."

It is along that way and that alone—the affectionate, respectful, and sympathetic interest in the religious life and worship of those who differ from us and those not in communion with us, that unity lies, and I feel sure there is no other. The religious life of a man, or people, is his life as it is influenced by the creed he professes and the worship he offers.

We are not thinking at the moment of a moral life, for a moral life is led by many who, as they would express it, "make no religious profession." It is open to us to question whether they are not more influenced than they are aware by the religion of those about them, which is in the very air they breathe, for there is such an influence as "religious atmosphere"; or we may think also that they have more religion than they suspect; but they themselves would disclaim all this. Some live, as John Stuart Mill lived, frankly without religion, yet leading a blameless and irreproachable moral life. Then as a contrast there are the lives of religious people leaving as far as moral values are concerned much to be desired, and probably, in many cases, most of all by themselves.

Religious life, however, is creed and worship translated into daily life and expression, effort and achievement; and accepting that definition I unhesitatingly claim for the Russian people that they are one of the most religious peoples in the world. Their religion is the desire and effort to know GOD. "This is life eternal, to know GOD, and JESUS CHRIST Whom He has sent." The Russian has not been fully taught as yet the ethical and moral side of this knowing GOD, though he is ready for it, but only its mystical side. He seeks the knowledge of GOD, quite simply, as a spiritual experience.

It will always be found that when races have received civilization and Christianity suddenly, as the Russians have done, while they astonish and charm by their spiritual fervour and deep earnestness, they disappoint by their want of consistency in moral life. But spiritual fervour and great earnestness arising out of a real need for GOD and a deep sense of His meeting that need "fulfilling minds and granting hearts' desires," and a real sense of communion with the Great Eternal in CHRIST in beautiful and uplifting worship, afford the best of all foundations for building up moral conduct permanently and well.

To the Russian, as to the ancient Hebrew, moral law will only lastingly and effectually appeal when prefaced by "GOD hath said." His religion is GOD; the knowledge of the Most High as revealed in CHRIST. And he is one of the most consistently religious persons in the world, for he must have his religion everywhere, and, just as the Hebrew felt it must be, "when talking with his children, when sitting in his house, when walking by the way, when going to lie down, and when rising up, written upon the posts of his house, and on the gates." The mystical or spiritual temperaments of the two peoples are much the same. Russians have a passion for GOD. They never want to be away from the sense and consciousness of His presence. Only when they have gained some sense of this spiritual endowment of the Russian race will my readers be able to see where their religious life corresponds with our own, and where it widely diverges from it. We have spoken of this war as a righteous war; the Russians as a religious one! They have brought their religion into it as they have never done into any war before. A Russian officer, for instance, gave a very picturesque account of the great battle of the Vistula last October, and ended with these words: "My company was the first to cross the river, which seemed to boil from the bursting of the shells. Afterwards nine companies rushed the enemy's position. A priest with long, streaming hair, and holding high a cross amid a hail of bullets, stood blessing the soldiers as they ran past." That is the true Russian, his religion everywhere and in everything. There is nothing in life, throughout the year, however secular it may seem to us to be, which does not have that blessing by the priest. The war has had it from first to last. All through mobilization, in the families from which the bread-winner was to go, there would be special little private services such as I have described in my last chapter. On the day when the conscripts were to depart from the village there would be the Liturgy in church, with all who could be present, and others outside. There would be, it has been described for us, the solemn reading of the Holy Gospel in the open-air, the book resting upon a living lectern; and as they rode away the last thing the departing men would see, as with those nine companies on the Vistula, would be the cross lifted high by a priest, with his long hair streaming over his shoulders, or out upon the wind.

It would be just the same all through the long journeys: the sacred *ikons* were carried, the priest marched steadily along, or sat in the railway carriages with the soldiers, and always with his cross. The soldiers of course saluted their priests as they saluted their officers, and for a time it was a little puzzling to decide how this salute should be suitably returned in such a war as this. For a priest to raise his hand to his cap did not seem to belong to his sacred office, and so it was decided he should touch his cross instead. Quite apart from the regular and official services, the priest would be always fulfilling his part in bringing God home to his countrymen, until the very end when he stood blessing them, as we have been told, as they rushed past him to attack, many of them to return no more. There is something very inspiring in the thought that the last earthly object many of them saw as they rushed on to death was the Cross of Him Who had robbed death of all its terrors, and brought Immortality to light.

One of my great reasons for looking to the Orthodox Church of Russia to give us our first opportunity, in seeking to promote the larger unity of Christendom, is, as I had occasion to say at a large public meeting in London last year, that, like ourselves, they wish to have the New Testament sense of the presence of CHRIST. I cannot use any other phrase to express my meaning. It is to me the whole spirit of their worship, not only at the Holy Communion, where one would expect it, but at all the other services as well. Litanies form a very important part of their worship, and as one hears that softly repeated "LORD, have mercy" (*Gospodi pomilui*) again and again from the choir, it is as if they were all conscious of speaking straight to their LORD with the feeling that He is there Himself to grant their prayer. No other refrain that I have ever heard has the same appealing note of real and moving faith.

I have attended the "all-night service" at S. Isaac's, in Petrograd, on Saturdays at 6 p.m. It lasts two hours in cathedrals and churches, but all night in monasteries and convents, and some of us going to S. Isaac's for the first time would almost wish that it could be "all night" there also. The glorious richness of the men's voices, their deep rolling basses and sweet tenors, the silvery trebles of the boys—there is no organ or other accompaniment—when heard as a new experience makes one involuntarily think to one's self "I have never heard prayer and praise expressed like this before." Whether one is behind the screen, where I was conducted at once, or standing with the choir before it—there are no seats in a Russian church—noting their picturesque uniforms like those of officers, and their profound reverence, or moving amongst the congregation, and looking towards the screen, the same impression is given everywhere and by every one, "We are praising Thee, O

GOD, we acknowledge Thee to be the LORD. Thou art the King of Glory, O CHRIST."

Interior of a Russian Church.

The screen separates the sacrarium from the body of the church, and is a carved partition painted and gilded, and in the cathedrals and great churches, is covered with silver and gold *ikons*, often richly jewelled, and with numerous lamps and tapers burning before them. At each side of this screen is a narrow door through which people seem to pass at will, to and fro, for there is a great feeling of freedom in a Russian church, and every one does just what he feels led to do. No ladies, however, may ever pass behind. In its centre are folding doors which are only used for ceremonial purposes, and are called "The Royal Gates." In the Liturgy it is a moment of deep solemnity when they are opened wide, and the priest passes through carrying the bread and wine for consecration. This is "The Great Entrance." At the evening service on Saturday night also there is an entrance, when the deacon carries the Gospels through, before which the gates stand open wide for a little while, and the congregation may look straight through. Immediately within stands the altar, a perfectly plain, square structure with nothing at all upon it but a large copy of the Four Gospels, and behind it is the seven-branched candlestick. It has an extraordinary effect upon the worshipper who has only just come to Russia when the Royal Gates are thrown open thus, and, with incense filling the air, the seven lamps on the great candlestick come into view. It is for a moment as if one was back in the days of Zacharias and Elisabeth, waiting for him to come forth through the gates to bless us, as he did on that memorable occasion after the announcement of the birth of S. John the Baptist. It is, however, only for a moment that the Temple fills the mind, for on looking up the representation of our LORD is there in the great window above, where He seems to look down upon us in love and blessing, and "The same yesterday, to-day, and for ever," seems to have new and blessed significance.

Russian worship to me is just dominated by the very presence of CHRIST. All the meretricious surroundings, the lights and glittering and jewelled *ikons* have not the least power to diminish the joyous, thankful sense of it. He is in the midst of us "gathered together in His Name." Every one seems to feel it, every one seeks to realize it. They are there for that! That is why the beautiful voices keep singing "*Gospodi pomilui*" or "LORD, be merciful to us." We feel it is real worship, and I can only hope that many of my readers who have not had the joy of it in that special way may yet have the opportunity afforded them. There are Russian churches, of course, in England, and I have happily and helpfully worshipped in the Russian church in Paris at 6 p.m. on Saturdays; but Russian worship can only be truly known and fully shared in Russia.

This "New Testament sense of the presence of CHRIST," as I have called it, is no doubt promoted by the extraordinary veneration given to the Gospels, both in their external and internal form. There is an intense feeling of close personal attention as the deacon carries them through the Royal Gates. They are always beautifully bound, rimmed and clasped with gold or silver, and often sparkling with diamonds and other precious stones. A beautifully bound copy—in ordinary churches the best they have—rests upon the altar, in its very centre, with a silken covering, and when the priest comes to celebrate he first kisses it, and then, lifting it up and setting it upon end, and laying the corporal where it has rested, with the chalice and paten upon it, proceeds to the Liturgy. The consecration takes place on that part of the altar where the Gospels have lain before, and where they will again be laid when the service is over.

The four evangelists always appear painted upon the Royal Gates, together with a representation of the Annunciation, our LORD, and the Holy Virgin, on either side. This is never departed from. In every church which follows traditional lines there are the four huge pillars holding up the whole structure—typifying the four evangelists again. Upon the roof they are set forth in the four cupolas, which are always there at the corners, while a fifth rising above them typifies our LORD over and above and dominating, yet supported by, them. Then there is nothing in the ordinary services to compare with the reading of the Holy Gospel to the people, nor is any special or private ministration complete without reading some portion of these, the most important parts of the sacred Scriptures.

It is easy to see, therefore, how it comes about that the Russian sense of the living CHRIST is essentially that which is realized by His Apostles and described in the New Testament.

Last year no less than three writers, as different from each other as they could well be, writing of visits paid to the Holy Land—Mr. Robert Hichens, the novelist, in *The Holy Land*, Sir Frederick Treves, the well-known and eminent surgeon, in *The Land that is Desolate*, and Mr. Stephen Graham, in *With the Russian Pilgrims to Jerusalem*—all alike show us that no one had made the same impression upon them as the Russians who had come to realize their LORD in the very place where He had lived our human life. They all so clearly felt that those simple-minded folk, as they followed traditions and visited one place after another from Bethlehem to Calvary, and wept where He had wept, and prayed where He had prayed, looked over the places and the waters upon which His eyes had rested, crossed themselves reverently again and again where He had suffered, and sung *Te Deum* and *Alleluia* where He had risen, were looking not at the things which are seen, but at the things which are not seen, believing with all the strength of their great and simple hearts that "the things which are seen are temporal, while the things which are not seen are eternal."

To the devout Russian the so-called good things of this life are unsubstantial and swiftly passing experiences, while the great and only realities worth thinking about seriously are those spiritual experiences of the Apostles as they went in and out with CHRIST and companied with Him, which are now described in the Gospels that we may have the same "even to the end of the ages." If Russia gives, as we pray she may, a lead to Christendom in the direction of unity, she will have a wonderfully uplifting and apostolic contribution to offer to the common stock of our Christian heritage.

And yet with all this wealth of very real spiritual experience there goes also a sad deficiency of moral conduct. "But that vitiates it all," some of my readers may exclaim. No; it does not. We, with our very different temperament, have come to substitute morality for religion and the ethical for the spiritual, whereas for the "whole man," as even Ecclesiastes tells us, *both* are necessary. Morality is not religion at all while the spiritual faculties are absolutely quiescent and the soul knows no need of GOD nor cries out for Him. A deep sense of the spiritual and a longing and effort to attain touch with the eternal is religion, although an imperfect morality impairs and cripples the adequate witness, the full unfettered enjoyment of it. And, as another writer has lately done in the political sphere, I would plead for the Russians that "they did not get a fair start."

I have already described the rough-and-ready way in which they were converted to Christianity, never having anything like our opportunities of instruction from the first. I have never heard a Russian sermon! The vast majority of the clergy have never been trained to preach, and would not be able to do so if they tried. The people are not taught at all in church, except by what is read to them in Scripture, or what they read for themselves. Let Englishmen give them "fair play" all round, both in political and constitutional, and also in moral deficiencies; and let us remember that it was to a body of real and earnest Christians—"saints" and "faithful," he himself calls them—that S. Paul found it necessary to write and caution against "the lusts of the flesh, foolish talking and unseemly jesting, covetousness and uncleanness, lying and stealing." If it was necessary to write those fifth and sixth chapters of the Ephesians to a body of Christian believers of whose sincerity an Apostle had no doubt, we may well have hopeful patience with a great body of our fellow Christians whose want of consistency in conduct provokes such ready criticism. It is well known how a mystical people like the West Indians (I have described it at length in a former book, *A Bishop among Bananas*, in chap. v) resent being accused of theft when helping themselves to "GOD'S gifts," as they call them, in the shape of fruit and fowls, when they would not dream of taking money, clothing, or other material things, or would consider themselves thieves if they did. And so it interested me to learn the other day that the Russian peasant views thefts of the same kind of things in much the same way, drawing in his mind a distinction between that which GOD gives for all and that which man produces for himself. It is imperfect reasoning, we know, as there is no real distinction between what a man produces by cultivation and what he manufactures; but we can understand an untrained and rather childlike mind making such a distinction.

The devout Russian peasantry in this stage often seem to illustrate our LORD'S words concerning things revealed to "babes" which even the "wise and prudent" seem to miss. Sir Donald M. Wallace again tells the story in *Our Russian Ally* which he told in his *Russia*—it will bear constant repetition—as an instance of real spiritual insight in a simple and untrained mind. "I remember once asking a common labourer," he says, "what he thought of the Mussulman Tartars among whom he happened to be living; and his reply, given with evident sincerity, was—'Not a bad sort of people.' 'And what about their religion?' I inquired. 'Not at all a bad sort of faith—you see they received it like the colour of their skins, from GOD.'" He assumed, of course, in his simple piety, that whatever comes from GOD must be good. It necessitated a very special spiritual experience and real vision before a Christian Apostle could say the same thing, "Of a truth I perceive that GOD is no respecter of persons"; but that common labourer in this little incident had taken in the same wide outlook, in a perfectly normal way, from his ordinary surroundings and the religious influences which make up such an important portion of his life.

The lesson is learnt early. I was, one morning, in an elementary school in Siberia, just before the work of the day began, to speak to the children. They opened with prayer, but how different from prayers in our own schools! The master and teachers did nothing except pray with the rest. At a sign that all was ready a boy of twelve stepped out and took his place before the *ikon* in its corner, and then bowing with that inimitable grace which belongs alone to the Russian when at prayer, and making the sign of the Cross, he gravely led the simple prayers of the whole school, all singing softly and reverently in unison. It was all inexpressibly touching and appealing, and to be treasured up with those other things of which one says, "I shall never forget."

The sign of the Cross is always made very slowly and solemnly, quite differently from other Churches, and from right to left upon the breast, and it is always accompanied by a slow and reverent bowing of the head, and is repeated usually three times. It is the special sign during the public services that a worshipper is just then feeling his or her own part in it. People do not use this devotion at set times during service, but just when they wish, and as the spirit moves them. I have been in the S. Isaac's choir when all the men and boys were singing a hymn, and suddenly a man near me would stop, bow, and cross himself devoutly, and then resume his hymn. No one would take the least notice, but all would go on singing as before. Then a choir-boy, after a moment or two, would do the same, his companions continuing to sing till their turn of being moved within came also. I have seen soldiers in the ranks do just the same when bareheaded at an outdoor service. There is so much spontaneity and elasticity and liberty in Russian worship. They do just as they feel "led by the Spirit" to do.

The Cathedral at Riga.

One of the most interesting experiences I had last year was attending on the Feast of the Epiphany—the appointed day for that and similar services—the blessing of the Neva. The ceremony takes place just outside the Winter Palace at Petrograd. Diplomatists and other visitors who wish to look on, stand within at the windows, but I much preferred to be outside, even though it was bitterly cold and we had to be bareheaded. There was a magnificent and bewildering gathering of Russian ecclesiastics, gorgeously vested. Priceless *ikons* were carried, and beautiful banners of rich embroideries, the whole effect being strangely Eastern in character. A few only could enter the small *kiosk* on the river's bank where the water, brought in a silver basin, was blessed. But the thrilling thing that day was the glorious singing, chant and refrain, which so richly filled the air, stirring the very depths of one's being, and the innumerable rows of deeply attentive soldiers in their long grey coats, whose frequent bowings and devout crossings all through the ranks showed that, though they were there officially, they were there to worship also. The Emperor walked from the palace amongst others and returned to it, bareheaded like any common soldier, with a perfectly plain overcoat like the rest, and nothing whatever to distinguish him from the crowd. He was unattended and moved quite freely with the rest, and could not be recognized except by a few of us standing near the door, who were already familiar with his appearance. There was but little cheering in consequence, though he acknowledged it in that modest and unaffected way which always distinguishes him. It was then that I saw the Grand Duke Nicholas for the first time, the generalissimo in the war, a magnificent man. He had certain announcements to make, or directions to give, and his grand voice rang out on the clear air so that every one could hear. "A real leader of men that," one felt instinctively without dreaming how soon one would have cause to remember the thought, under tragically altered circumstances.

We cannot possibly attach too much importance to the fact, admitted on all sides and in the most unexpected quarters, that this great race, coming so very closely into our lives, uniting their destiny in some measure with our own, is above all others a distinctly religious people. Russia, as must be ever becoming more and more evident, is to be our ally in a way hitherto entirely unknown to our race and nation. Thoughtful observers have seen it coming for some time, and are not taken at all by surprise, but the idea is still new and not altogether welcome to many. There is no doubt at all about it in my own mind, and I shall return to it more fully in a later chapter, that while we shall still remain the friends of France and act the part of true "friends in need" should occasion again arise, and look with a friendly eye upon other nationalities, and even—how much I hope it—make up our quarrel with Prussia and the German peoples she has influenced against us, yet with Russia our relations are already altogether different, and our two empires are rapidly beginning to realize that they are coming together in an entirely different relationship, to knit up true and enduring ties of brotherly unity with each other, not for selfish purposes at all, but for a great work together for civilization and for GOD. We Anglo-Saxons are a deeply religious people at heart, though with our temperamental reticence and reserve we speak least about the things of which we feel the most. The Russians are also a sincerely religious people, and they, on the other hand, bring out most readily, spontaneously, and naturally, the things which mean most to them. We are unlike each other in temperament, yet absolutely like each other in our view of the deep things of GOD. Thus complementary to one another, we have a real intelligible hope of a lasting friendship. We should have no hope at all of any such tie between ourselves and them if they did not share our serious view of human life and responsibility, and base that view upon a firm belief in GOD. We should feel at heart that we had no real confidence in their stability, grit, and powers of staying and lasting out.

Surely the one thing that has come out during the war is the supreme importance of *morale*. Napoleon went so far, I have seen it stated, as to say it counted for an army, in proportion to its numbers, as three to one. I remember too how the military correspondent of the *Times*, in one of his most interesting articles on the Balkan War, when it was drawing to a close, explained the disastrous defeat of the Turkish army by the gradual loss of *morale* they had sustained by the decay of religion amongst them under the régime of the Young Turks. Prayers had been largely given up by the troops, who no longer had the ministrations of their spiritual leaders, and *morale* had gone in consequence. Then had come disaster. He contrasted with all this the tremendous fervour of the Balkan League, and described a picture he had recently seen in a French illustrated paper. Two French officers were shown looking at a Bulgarian regiment on their knees, their priest praying for them and blessing them before they went into action. "What would one of our generals get," said one of the French officers to his friend, "if he ordered such a thing as that?" "He would get the victory," quietly said the other.

I am expecting great things from Russia, and for us through Russia, for civilization and for GOD, and what I have written is being ever more and more widely felt by others also, and even expressed in daily papers, where at one time we should not have expected such a thing to be thought of in the midst of a great war. "That Russia is one of the most truly religious countries in the world is proved by the crowds which filled and overflowed in all the churches yesterday when thanksgiving services were held in celebration of the victory, *nor is it possible to doubt the sincerity and devotion* of the worshippers. The firm belief in the divine ruling of the world is to be found among *all classes*."[7]

FOOTNOTES:

[7] *The Daily Mail* correspondent at Petrograd, November 12, 1914.

CHAPTER VI
HIS IMPERIAL MAJESTY THE TSAR

One interesting figure has held the attention of the Continent of Europe for many long years, appealing to the imagination and baffling comprehension, but will never fill the same place again. Another, however, is coming forward very possibly in his stead, without any wish or intention of his own, and that other is the Emperor of Russia. He will do so, I believe, just as the German Emperor has done, because history affords him the opportunity, and because, like the Kaiser, he too is a man who cherishes thoughts of great purposes for his people and ideals for himself.

It affords me the greatest pleasure to write about the Emperor—he is not usually spoken of in Russian society as the Tsar—for I shall always feel most deeply grateful to him for his great personal kindness at my first audience with him, and the great encouragement he gave me at the very beginning of my work abroad.

Her Imperial Majesty the Tsaritsa.

I have already explained the quaking spirit in which I crossed the frontier. It so happened that Russia was the first country I visited when appointed to take charge of the jurisdiction, and, as to so many others, there was something forbidding to me in the very name of Russia. I knew at that time also that my visitations would bring me, as they have done, into contact with other sovereigns, and with great personages in other countries, and here at St. Petersburg I was to begin with the most unknown and, as one thought of his vast empire, most overwhelming of them all. And then—but let me describe an audience at the palace at Tsarskoe Selo, for it will probably interest many a reader, and also explain how very different from a somewhat perturbed anticipation was the pleasurable reality. I have taken care to satisfy myself beforehand that I shall not be transgressing any of the rules of court etiquette, nor be guilty of any breach of confidence in so doing.

Audiences abroad are always arranged through the British Embassy or Legation. Court dress is worn in Russia, even though the reception itself is perfectly informal, but, as court dress for a bishop consists in being robed as for Easter services, in red chimere, etc., there was no difficulty in providing it even for one who has to carry everything in a couple of bags, and for months at a time.

Tsarskoe Selo—"The Tsar's village," the words mean—is a little over half an hour by rail from Petrograd, and I was instructed to start from the Imperial Station in Petrograd, and there walked over rich carpets, through saluting soldiers, to the imperial train, most beautifully and comfortably arranged with smoking, writing, and reading compartments. Upon arrival at Tsarskoe Selo imperial carriages are always waiting for those expected, with coachman and footman on the box, wearing bright scarlet cloaks edged with white fur and very smart cocked hats of red and gold.

It was a typical Russian wintry day with a tremendous blizzard blowing, and blinding snow falling. Sentries were stationed at intervals through the streets of the village, saluting all the imperial carriages as they went by, although no occupant could be seen; and having passed through it we entered the park and soon drew up at the door of the small palace where the Emperor always resides, and which, white itself, looked that day like a fairy palace rising up amid the snow.

Nothing could be more strikingly different from that white world without, however, than the warmth and richness of colour within. On every side there were brilliant and unfamiliar liveries and dazzlingly rich uniforms. An official, of huge physique, wearing several medals, with a broad gold band round his head, from which, on its right side, stuck out a curious bunch of dark feathers, in velvet and lace dress, and with breeches and silk stockings—there was no one the least like him in the crowd of attendants—at once came forward and led me away to a dressing-room in which to leave my furs and change into my robes. He then conducted me through one beautiful room after another, each one richly furnished and adorned with beautiful china, paintings, *ikons*, trophies, and presents from different parts of the empire, until at length we reached a small room where a number of officers in brilliant uniforms were seated and evidently in attendance.

One of them, the Conte de Grabbé, at once came forward and welcomed me, chatting pleasantly until a servant, very quietly attired like an English butler, came out from a room opposite and, holding the door open, signified that I was to enter.

There was no introduction or announcement of any kind, and, as I entered, the Emperor was already standing there to meet me, smiling pleasantly and encouragingly, with extended hand.

"It is very kind in your Imperial Majesty," I said, "to allow me to come and see you in this informal way."

"It is very kind in you to come and see us, bishop," he replied, so cheerily and unaffectedly, that away went every bit of diffidence and sense of constraint, and, to my great relief and gratitude, I found myself talking as naturally as to an intimate friend. I say "gratitude" because, being put so entirely at ease, able to say all that it was in my mind to say, and ask anything that it was in my mind to wish to know, enabled me to get a clear idea of the Emperor's attractive personality, and even, as he spoke quite freely, of some at least of the opinions and principles which must rule his conduct and shape his policy and government.

"He gives you confidence," a diplomatist who had had many official audiences with him said to me one day, and that exactly describes the effect he produces. He talked freely of all things before the public mind just then— of the approaching Coronation of King George, for whom he expressed a more than cousinly regard and respect; of domestic duties and family life as the ideals which shape the destinies of races; of the Russian Church, particularly asking if its dignitaries had welcomed me; of our English Church; of travelling; of my own impressions of Russia and other things. It was quite astonishing afterwards to recall the ground we had covered in that interview. And before I left he inquired:—

"When will you be coming to Russia again, bishop?"

"Next year, sir," I said; "for I believe I am to go to Siberia."

"Siberia! How interesting! I've never yet been to Siberia. Then you'll come and tell us all about it when you return, won't you?"

"I shall be much honoured, sir." And praying God's blessing upon himself and the imperial family, for which he thanked me as simply and modestly as any other layman would have done, I withdrew, feeling that it had been one of the most helpful and memorable interviews I had ever had.

I have been often asked if the Emperor is not very much like our King, and it is a somewhat difficult question to answer. As he stood there that morning, in a simple pale blue uniform, well set up and looking extraordinarily young and boyish, and smilingly happy—so entirely different from one's expectations—it did not occur to me to see any such likeness, but an old courtier said to me, in speaking after luncheon of "the resemblance which is so much talked of"—

"There is no resemblance to be noticed when their two Majesties are together, nor would there be any striking likeness seen between their portraits in colours, but in photographs or anything that is black and white, just bringing out light and shade, then the similarity is most remarkable, you might easily mistake one for the other."

This puts one's own impressions very clearly. There is a well-known photograph, circulated as a postcard in Germany, and from a German negative, of which I have a copy, in which the two Emperors are shown in conversation on the imperial yacht. Any one seeing it in English hands would certainly think that it was our King and the Kaiser, and be quite astonished at learning it was not.

The Emperor received me the first time in a very comfortable but simply furnished study, and the last time, when, in accordance with his invitation, I went to tell him about my two missions to Siberia, in his billiard-room fitted up as a study or library, and in which he led me to the kind of window-seat which we know so well in English country houses, looking out upon the park. Afterwards luncheon was served for me in the *Grand Palais* of the Great Catherine, a most magnificent and immense palace a little distance away, full of interesting souvenirs of Russia's past.

His Imperial Highness the Tsarevitch Alexei.

It is well known how many and different rumours have been circulated during the last two years about the heir to the throne, and it seems rather a pity that the simple truth has not been announced and made fully known from the first, for I am assured on the best authority in Petrograd, that the Tsarevitch suffers from a skin affection not unknown, unfortunately, to members of our royal family, which, as he is a very high-spirited boy, difficult to watch and caution, has in moments of exuberance and violent exertion caused him to receive injuries which for a time have been disabling.

When last at Tsarskoe Selo, before taking my leave I took out some puzzles from my pocket, made of wood and steel, quite inexpensive, as I thought it likely they would be most welcome because most unfamiliar, and handing them to the Emperor, said:—

"I have brought the Tsarevitch a present, sir, and I bring it out with much hesitation, for it is a very simple one, and I know he must have had many beautiful and costly gifts this Christmas."

"Not at all," he said; "we bring him up very simply, and he loves puzzles. He and I used up all we could get, especially those jig-saw puzzles, while he was ill. These, I see, are new."

"I hope," I said, "that he is now better?"

"Yes," he said, "he is; he's quite well now—quite well," he repeated with emphasis.

The Emperor speaks English perfectly, fluently, and with ease, and I have been told that it is the language most generally, if not always, used in the ordinary daily life of the imperial family.

I have taken up some time in giving these personal impressions, but I think it is quite worth while to do so just now as the Emperor was so particularly gracious and kind, and thus enabled me to form some idea of what he is, just as a man and a father in his own home; and that I know will appeal to my own countrymen when wondering what is likely to be his policy and aim as a ruler of a vast empire.

A man can only *do* what he *is*, whether he be in the highest or the lowest positions in the world; and he always brings out, sooner or later, what he is at heart. It must therefore be a very great source of confidence to us all just now, when we believe that the providence of GOD has brought the British and the Russian Empires together, not for temporary, but for enduring objects, to know, as I feel we may consider that we do know, that the Emperor of all the Russias is a man we can all respect and trust, precisely as we respect and trust our own Sovereign—as one whose ideals are those of domestic duty and family life on the one hand, and the real interests and well-being of the labouring and toiling millions of his people on the other.

A somewhat scandalous book was written last year which I won't mention by name, lest curiosity should lead those who have not read it to do so, which gave a most unfavourable impression of the Emperor and the imperial family. It was not, however, written by an Englishman; and, without questioning in any way the writer's *bona fides*, I am bound to say, and very confidently and energetically, that I have never yet met one of my own countrymen who has had to do with the Emperor of Russia, financially, diplomatically, or in audience, who has not expressed himself to me about him in the same appreciative terms as I have here used myself.

Take, for instance, what Sir Donald Mackenzie Wallace has written only a few months ago.[8] "The antiquated idea that Tsars are always heartless tyrants who devote much of their time in sending troublesome subjects to Siberia, is now happily pretty well exploded, but the average Englishman is still reluctant to admit that an avowedly autocratic government may be, in certain circumstances, a useful institution. There is no doubt, however, that in the gigantic work of raising Russia to her present level of civilization, the Tsars have played a most important part. As for the present Tsar, he has followed, in a humane spirit, the best traditions of his ancestors. Any one who has had opportunities of studying closely his character and aims, and who knows the difficulties with which he has had to contend, can hardly fail to regard him with sympathy and admiration. Among the qualities which would commend him to Englishmen are his scrupulous honesty and genuine truthfulness. Of these—were I not restrained by fear of committing a breach of confidence—I might give some interesting illustrations.

"As a ruler, Nicholas II habitually takes a keen, sympathetic interest in the material and moral progress of his country; and is ever ready to listen attentively and patiently to those who are presumably competent to offer sound advice on the subject. At the same time he is very prudent in action; and this happy combination of zeal and caution, which distinguishes him from his too impetuous countrymen, has been signally displayed in recent years. During the revolutionary agitation which followed close on the disastrous Japanese War, when the impetuous would-be reformers wished to overturn the whole existing fabric of administration, and the timid counsellors recommended vigorous retrograde measures, he wisely steered a middle course, which has resulted in the creation of a moderate form of parliamentary institutions."

I am not alone, therefore, in the very favourable impression I have formed of the Russian Emperor as a man whom the best of my own countrymen may respect as one like-minded with themselves in his views of life and conduct, and his own countrymen thoroughly trust as a constitutional ruler who, though determined, as he will be advised by his most trusted counsellors, to go cautiously, yet is convinced that a good government's one and chief concern is the well-being of those who are governed, and especially of those who form the lowest class in its social scale.

Like Sir Donald Wallace, I too could give instances of the Emperor's straightforward and generous action which show the essential right-mindedness of his nature in a very striking way, if it were possible to do so without breach of confidence. Especially was this the case in a particular instance of which I know, when it was a question of putting his own interests, and even dignity, in a very secondary position. It was one, indeed, in which no great ruler could be expected or asked to do so, but when he learnt himself what was involved he at once did so subordinate his own interests, and has earned in consequence the lasting gratitude of all concerned, and their entire and loyal confidence.

The Russian people are intensely loyal, and, as the overwhelming majority are of the peasant class, their loyalty is of that simple, fervid, and trusting character which is seen in their family and village life. They do not speak of the "Emperor" so much as of "The Little Father," and that is how they feel towards him. He is the father of his people and they are his children. If there is anything they object to in legislation it is always put down to officialdom, just as our own Colonies, before the days when they began to "think imperially," used to vent all their displeasure upon "Downing Street" when unwelcome legislation took place, and never upon Queen Victoria (or her government), for whom they had the greatest respect and affection. The Russian peasant too murmurs loudly at times against the governors and their subordinates when he is requested to do something that he does not like, but with a solacing reflection to himself that "The Little Father would put everything right if he only knew."

There is disaffection and serious disloyalty in other quarters, and I shall try my best to describe it and what may very possibly be some of its causes, in my chapter on "Russia's Problem," but the dangerous disaffection, probably already beginning to pass away, is confined to a few of the largest towns, and does not in any way affect the overwhelming majority of the Emperor's subjects, who are entirely devoted to him and patriotically loyal.

This ought to be remembered also when we are thinking over future relations between our own people and theirs. The Russians are not a downtrodden and oppressed people struggling to throw off the yoke of a harsh and despotic rule, but are contented, loyal, and law-abiding. They do not, however, show their loyalty by any outward expressions such as the "All Highest," and others with which we have been made familiar in the addresses and letters of Germans of high rank, office, and birth, during the war. No such terms exist or are thought of amongst the subjects of the Emperor of Russia. The word Tsar occurs, I believe, in the National Anthem, and Tsaritsa is used occasionally, while there is no such word as Tsarina in the language. But neither Tsar, Emperor, Tsaritsa, or Empress are used, I am told, amongst the ordinary people. They speak of *"Gosudar"* and *"Gosudarina"* which mean Lord and Lady, or Sir and Madame, and in such general use are these terms, I believe, that a man writing a business letter to a tradesman would begin "Gracious Gosudar." The Tsarevitch Alexis is spoken of amongst the people by a word in perfectly common use, which is no more than the ordinary word for "heir." Loyalty and great respect, it would seem, are quite consistent with great familiarity of thought and expression.

The Emperor is probably spoken of more frequently as Nicolai Alexandrovitch—"Nicholas, son of Alexander"—than by any other title, and I feel sure that the Grand Duke Nicholas, Commander-in-Chief, and his doings at head-quarters, have been spoken of all over Russian plains and Siberian steppes this winter as familiarly and as proudly as of some one who had gone from their own village. "Ah! Nicolai Nicolaievitch! What a man he is! How well he has fought this war! How proud we are of him!" etc., etc. I was told lately of a touching incident which occurred at a great service in Russia (the translation of the remains of a great saint) at which the Grand Duchess Serge was present, and, when she arrived, had gone quietly up to a gallery pew, arranged for her and other great ladies. Soon afterwards an old peasant woman, to whom she had once shown a kindness, arrived, and at once began to inquire:—

"Has Elizabeth come yet?"—the Grand Duchess's Christian name—"I want Elizabeth. She told me when next I came where she was to be sure and ask for her. Where's Elizabeth?"

The Grand Duchess in her exalted gallery caught something of what was going on, and, hearing her own name, at once came down.

"Here I am, little mother!" And then with "Dear Elizabeth!" the old woman threw her arms about her neck and began her story.

Such a thing is only possible in Russia, and yet it is the one country in the world where we have always been led to think that between the highest and the lowest there is that "great gulf fixed," which if not bridged over in this life by sympathy and love, has little hope of being passed in the world to come.

Rank and position and high office if worthily filled need no buttressing up. Least of all need those who hold them give themselves airs. Their office is enough in itself; and last year, when I had a large party of German youths to take about London, and by the kindness of those concerned took them to see one or two great places where they were most courteously and graciously received—they were the sons of working men in Frankfurt—I was more than pleased to hear one of them say to his friend, "I notice that in England the higher the rank the less the pretence." So it is in Russia. The more exalted the position the more unaffected and simple the one who fills it!

The Grand Duchess Elizabeth, daughter of our own Princess Alice, is probably the best known and the best loved woman in all Moscow, indeed in all Russia, and hereafter will, in all probability, have "Saint" prefixed to her name. Many do not hesitate to use it even now. Her sad experiences appealed most powerfully to the people's sympathies when she was so tragically widowed a few years ago. Her husband, the Grand Duke Serge,

Governor of Moscow, had become extremely unpopular with certain classes, and it was well known that his life was in danger; but he knew no fear, and drove out constantly in an open carriage in which the Grand Duchess insisted upon accompanying him. It is said that at length a letter was written to him advising him to leave her behind if he valued her life, and adding significantly, "We have no quarrel with her, nor anything against her." She was, therefore, from that time left at home, his secretary asking to be allowed to go in her place. Again the same kind of letter was received, and he too was left behind; and the Grand Duke, who was no coward, determined to go alone. And then, on the first morning he did so, and not far from his own door, the fatal bomb was thrown, and did its work so effectually that there was nothing left to be seen! He was literally "blown to atoms." Every one in Moscow is said to have heard the terrific explosion, and knew at once. "They have him at last!" The Grand Duchess heard also and rushed immediately to the scene. It may be questioned whether any other woman has ever had such an ordeal as that to face! She had just seen her husband drive away from his home, and in a few moments there was nothing left! I believe a finger with his signet ring was subsequently found, but that was all.

Moscow, which had always respected and admired her, at once gave her whole-hearted sympathy, which soon became a deep and true affection as they learnt that she had determined to give her whole life and income to their poor.

She founded the first order which has been introduced into Russia for women's work amongst the sick and poor. When I was last in Moscow, she explained to me its character, and it seemed to me to be a blend of the Tertiaries of S. Francis and the deaconesses of the primitive church, though the latter is the model she has wished to follow. She told me she had ninety-six sisters in the order now, and that whilst some sick were brought into their own wards many were visited in their own homes. It is this visiting work that she hopes most to develop as time goes on. She is, of course, by Baptism and Confirmation a member of our own Church, and is full of interest and sympathy towards it, and usually attends the Abbey service when in London, though she joined the Orthodox Church of Russia during her married life. This, she told me, was without any influence being brought to bear upon her, and entirely from conviction that it was best for her own religious life in her adopted country.

She wore the simple and grey habit of her order, and it was difficult to realize that she was a princess of the blood, and sister-in-law to the Emperor himself, as she spoke so simply and humbly about her work, and what she hoped still with the blessing of GOD to do. She does not cut herself off, however, from life's ordinary relationships, for when later at Tsarskoe Selo,

I told the Emperor that I had been able to see her and hear about her work, he said, "She is coming to spend a fortnight with us this very afternoon."

That is what one meets everywhere in Russia, the unconventional and the natural. The superior of a new order, which is an entirely fresh departure, would be expected in any other country to give up everything else in the way of social and family relationships. But in Russia, if a perfectly natural thing like a visit to near relations suggests itself as desirable the visit is duly paid.

It is so always! The splendid and the simple, high rank and humble birth seem to find themselves close together, the rich and the poor unite so easily in a common interest. "A gorgeous imperial procession was passing through the palace hall," writes one who saw it at Tsarskoe Selo as a specially grand function, "and two or three maid-servants appeared at the head of a little staircase to look on, wearing print dresses. No one told them to go away."[9] No one would think of it.

The Emperor loves the simple folk he governs, and showed it plainly when in the earlier part of his reign he moved freely amongst them, standing next to peasants and workmen in Moscow, when he stepped into a church to pray. And after he returned from our own country, from the marriage of King George, I read the other day, "somebody asked him what had impressed him most. 'The crowd outside Buckingham Palace waiting to see Queen Victoria drive out,' he said. 'There they waited, hour after hour, and at last a little black carriage came out of the palace-gates. Very few of the people in the crowd could see the Queen, but they knew that she was there, and they went away satisfied. One day it will be like that in Russia.'" And the writer adds: "I do not think the Emperor's prophecy is likely to be realized in his lifetime; but a day will come when his subjects will forget the mistakes that have been made in his name, and recognize that they owe to him great reforms." I fancy in subsequent editions, for his book well deserves to have them, he will alter those words into "I feel sure that he will live to see it, and not have long to wait."

Her Imperial Highness the Grand Duchess Elizabeth—The Friend of the Poor.

FOOTNOTES:

[8] *Our New Ally.*

[9] Rothay Reynolds, *My Russian Year.*

CHAPTER VII
A PATERNAL GOVERNMENT

Two years ago, when I was in conversation with one of our leading diplomatists, who has a very intimate knowledge of the Russian people, their Emperor and governing classes, I asked him, "Do you not think that the Russian government is the most paternal in its aim and character of all the governments in Europe?"

"Of course I do," he replied; and rather excitedly added, "But when I even hint at such a view of Russian methods to our own countrymen here at home they regard me as if I had taken leave of my senses, and look at me with an incredulous and pitying eye."

It is no wonder that this should be so when our own people still, for the most part, look upon Russia as the land of the knout and banishment, with an oppressive and despotic government which on the least suspicion seizes upon unoffending victims and consigns them to Siberia and the mines, where, chained together, they drag out their lingering existence in unfamiliar and degrading toil. No words are wasted, it is believed, upon the weak and ineffective, but the lash comes stingingly down upon their shoulders. Harsh legislation is the rule, it is thought, and if perchance people rise up in masses against it, as they do from time to time, the dreaded Cossack sweeps through the streets, and, at terrible cost to human life, clears them. Again and again I find this is the prevailing idea of Russia, as I am asked if I am not afraid to travel there; and something like it, I have candidly admitted, was my own impression before I went there and saw things for myself. But nothing could be more unlike the actual reality.

The relations of the governing and governed in Russia are really paternal on the one hand and filial on the other, and I hope that I may be able to induce my readers to believe that is true of the greater part of the whole population.

In the first place, the knout is long since gone. No such thing exists now, except as a curiosity, in the whole of Russia, nor has it been used officially since the days of the present Emperor's *great grandfather*!

Next there are the convicts. It is now twenty-five years since Mr. Harry de Windt, the well-known traveller, disproved the lurid accounts which had been given a short time before of the horrors of Siberian prisons. In his book of 1903 he says, "I have always maintained that were I sentenced to a term of penal servitude I would infinitely prefer to serve it in (some parts of) Siberia than in England." When he puts these words in brackets he is thinking, of course, of the severity of climate and distance from frequented routes, and not of the treatment of the prisoners. He tells at length—space does not permit me to quote freely as I would like to do—how even criminal convicts are well cared for; and that even the murderers and murderesses amongst them, for there is no capital punishment in Russia, are lodged in wards which are clean and well warmed; that there is a comfortable infirmary connected with a prison, and even a home close at hand, supported by private subscription, for children of the prisoners.

Mr. Foster Fraser also, in his book on *The Real Siberia*—perhaps one of the best known of modern works on that part of the empire—tells us that having been more "thrilled" as a boy by what he had read about Siberian prisons than by Red Indian stories, and knowing that people, the world over, were in the habit of saying, "Only Russia could be so cruel, a civilized country would shrink from such barbarities," determined to go and see for himself, and, as is usual with those who go to Russia full of prejudice and dread, the scales fell from his eyes when he visited Irkutsk prison. He found to his surprise that, "It was not the gloomy, sullen-stoned, slit-windowed, iron-barred structure such as are our prisons at home"; and he describes at length a system which will compare favourably with any other prisons in the world, as to discipline, but surpasses them all in friendliness and freedom from constraint. "What attracted me was the informal relationship between governor and prisoners. The men talked without any restraint, made requests and even jests." But the climax of his experiences of "Siberian horrors" came when he asked to see the women prisoners, and was taken to the "best house in the place," where, on going into the yard, he saw some women "sitting about, and some children playing with a kitten."

"I'll send for the matron," said the governor.

"Is this the prison?" I asked in some amazement.

"Yes—this is the only prison we have in Irkutsk for women."

"It was just a large-sized ordinary house," he goes on, "abutting on the street, but not a single soldier to see. I couldn't help laughing," he adds, for the women, who numbered about forty, and had twenty children with them, represented offences which ranged from petty theft up to murder, the five or six murderesses being much the same as the others in appearance and character as far as could be seen. Mr. Fraser felt it was absurd to call such a place a prison, and asked:—

"Do you really mean to say that these women don't go away?"

And then his amazement was complete when he was told that one had surprised them very much, a little while before, by going off, but had surprised them even more by coming back after a day or two and telling them that she had wanted to see a man she was rather fond of and have a week-end with him, as men visitors were not allowed on Sundays, the visiting day!

It will be conceded, I think, by my most prejudiced reader, that Russia does not seem to be unduly harsh in her dealings with even her worst type of criminals!

Next let me speak of "politicals," as we may call them. It is nearly two years ago since a meeting was organized in London to protest in the name of civilization—very strong language indeed was used in the preliminary circular—against Russia's treatment of her political prisoners; and one who holds very high office in London, and whom it was specially desired to have present, did me the honour of asking my advice about attending it, as I had just returned from Siberia. I replied at once, and pointed out how very difficult and delicate the work of embassies and legations is made when such meetings of protest are held in the countries they represent, and that we should deeply resent meetings of a similar kind being held in other countries with respect to methods of our own. We are open to criticism ourselves at times, every one will admit! I gave it as my opinion also that the statements of the circular were greatly exaggerated. Wishing later to be assured that this was so, I questioned a Russian of high rank in diplomacy, who at once said:—

"Suppose you go and see for yourself the next time you are in Siberia. Visit any mines you wish, or prisons either, and the Russian government shall afford you all facilities."

Characteristic Group of Russians.

This I am hoping to do this very year, if all's well, and so, though I have seen convicts for myself in Siberia, yet what I have to say here now is not at first hand, but still it will be on the best authority in every case, and when I can I will give names. It was quite a revelation to me as I listened, on my first visit to Russia, to the statements I heard on all sides whenever banishment to Siberia was mentioned.

"But surely you know what that means? No? Well, for ordinary political offenders who are either suspect or actually giving offence, and making government difficult, all that it means is that they have to go and live in Siberia, where their wives and families follow them. Their property is not seized nor income forfeited. It can all be realized, and so they can live as comfortably there as in Russia. There are people indeed who prefer to live in Siberia after they have gone there. After a few years or so, if they like to escape they can do so, and no one interferes. They can live where they please, but they must not return to Russia."

That did not seem a very hard fate, nor can it be said to be a very undeserved one, for every one must feel that the government of a country so vast is beset with difficulties and must, in the present state of its population, be firm, and not hesitate at strong measures against those plotting against it. I know myself, in a recent case too, which caused much excitement in this country, warning after warning was given to enable the offender to leave the country before arrest took place, and even after the sentence unexpected indulgence and clemency were shown.

Let me now quote straight from Mr. Foster Fraser's book, written by one who tells us frankly that he "went to Siberia with the average Britisher's prejudice against things Russian, but with eyes open," and determined to see things for himself.

"The political prisoners are given the best part of the country to live in, namely, in the west. Other prisoners are exiled nearer to the icy regions according to the gravity of their offence. The political prisoners may practise handicrafts, and, by special permission, medicine. A 'political' is not identified with the criminal any more than a debtor is identified with a felon in England. Such offenders do not travel with other prisoners in a gang. A 'political' may be on a train going into exile; but no one knows it besides himself and the members of the police travelling in the same carriage. Politicals get about £1. 10s. a month from the government, but this varies according to the district to which they are sent. Wives who accompany their husbands are allowed 36 lb. of bread a month, but must submit to the regulations of the *étape*. If all goes well with a 'political' he gets permission to settle in some Siberian town with his family, but any allowance from the government then ceases. He is just the same as any other resident, save that he can never leave Siberia. If he wishes to farm, the government will give him a plot of land and money to work it. But this money must be paid back by instalments." He states, as will be seen, "he can never leave Siberia," but what, I fancy, was really meant by his informant was "never return to Russia." We can hardly think, in a land where the executive is so indulgent as to allow a dangerous criminal to "week-end" with a friend, that they will be less considerate to a political of good character wishing to go to a better climate and letting it be understood that Russia would not be the place selected. There is the human touch about everything in that country of spacious and large ideas, and it is not lacking either in the treatment of political offenders or with other criminals and felons also.

Mr. Harry de Windt is not only explicit but even amusing and entertaining as he tells us what he found at Yakutsk, which is quite remote enough from civilization, on the great Lena post road, to make one feel that the lot of the banished there must be sad indeed; but at the same time we can enter a little, perhaps, into his feelings of amazement when he found that "the political exiles there seemed to be no worse off, socially, than any one else, for they moved about in society and were constantly favoured guests of the Chief of Police. The exiles, however, were not permitted to take part in the private theatricals I have mentioned, a restriction which caused them great annoyance. Their loud and unfavourable criticisms from the stalls on the evening in question were certainly not in the best of taste, and, to my surprise, they were not resented by the governor's staff." This incident will show that, in Yakutsk at any rate, the "politicals" are treated not only with leniency but with a friendly courtesy, which on this occasion was certainly abused. Mr. Olenin, an exile whose term of banishment was expiring, told me that he had no fault whatever to find with Yakutsk as a place of exile, so much so that he had resolved not to return to Russia at the end of his sentence, but to remain here and complete an ethnological work upon which he was engaged. I don't think that "harshness and barbarity" are words that can be appropriately used for a discipline that permits attendances at "private theatricals" where politicals are so much at ease that they indulge in loud and unfavourable criticisms in the presence of the governor's staff, and go out as favoured guests to dinner parties given by the Chief of the Police!

A few months ago, however, I had my last and great surprise as to Russia, in learning—what strangely enough is not yet known to many Russians of experience and official rank—that convict labour in mines is entirely abandoned now, and has been for some years! It was found to be both unprofitable and impracticable as modern ideas of mining advanced. It was clearly a great waste of time to march gangs to the "pit's mouth," as they call it in our own mining districts, and remove their chains before sending them down, putting them on when they came up again. Then no blasting is now done without dynamite; and that, clearly, was a dangerous substance to hand over to criminals. Again, they are of all classes, and but few could ever have worked in mines before, and not having either technical knowledge or experience, their work would be unprofitable. Convict labour below ground has been given up for some time in consequence. Prisoners now, when sent out to Siberia, are only required to work above ground, though they may go into the mines if they choose, and have fitness for the work, and can be trusted. They are all allowed and encouraged to hire themselves out, receiving the market price for their work, and so being able to obtain little comforts for themselves. As far as I have been able to consider the experiences of reliable authorities, I feel convinced that when able to see for myself I too shall say I would far rather serve a term of imprisonment with hard labour amongst the convicts of Siberia than in Dartmoor or Portland. There is far more of the human touch in the former, and a man does not suffer in his manhood in the same way there as he does in the English, French, Belgian, and Central American prisons I have known.

How, then, are we to account for all the well-known stories of miseries and sufferings associated with that lone, and in winter very terrible land? Most of us read in our youthful days *Elizabeth, or the Exiles of Siberia*, and since then have always spoken of "the Siberian mines," and "banishment" with bated breath! How have such impressions so gained ground that the very name of Russia has taken us straightway out of Europe into Asia to thoughts of the severest and most hopeless criminal punishments in the world? I should say that the explanation is to be found, very possibly, in the methods used before arrest. What is called "administrative procedure" has long been the usual way of dealing with suspected political offenders. A man or woman is arrested, and without public trial is removed to Siberia, and there required to live under police supervision. Arrests are made at any time. "A man may be seated quietly at home with his family, in his office, or at some place of public entertainment, when a touch upon his shoulder summons him away." There are no press reports of his trial or examination, which is conducted in private, nor any appeal from it, and there have been, and perhaps are still, cases where a suspected offender's family remain in ignorance of what has happened to him, or where he is. The thought of such a disappearance from the midst of family and friends is enough to chill any heart, and even if Russia does consider it necessary to deal thus summarily with those who are enemies of social order and the well-being of the State, without being unduly harsh in her treatment of them when they are exiled, one may very well hope that what have been called the "underground methods" of her police may soon be entirely laid aside. It is still consistent, I submit, with the aim of a paternal government to remove at once, and with no uncertain or hesitating hand, those who are considered the most dangerous elements in its social life, and the enemies of its stability and well-being.

It was in Siberia, however, that I learnt the positive side of Russia's care for her peasant and working population. There I found, as soon as I looked into the working of a great company, that it was necessary to have a Russian engineer, in addition to the one employed by the staff, who is held responsible by the governor of the district for the inspection of all machinery and the arrangements made for securing those employed from unnecessary risk and danger. A police officer of a superior class is attached to the staff also, not only to maintain order, but to receive any complaints and transmit them if serious to higher authorities. The government distinctly interferes in order to guard the interests of its working class, and though sometimes the presence of another engineer or the police official may seem irksome, our countrymen recognize loyally that the government have no wish to be vexatious, but only to fulfil their duty to their own people.

Then next I found, also in Siberia, how extraordinarily kind and helpful all officials are to colonists, who are not always easy to deal with when travelling or settling down in a new country. They take things for granted and expect much, and yet are never disappointed; officials of every class, and especially on railways, being unfailing in patience, tact, good-nature, and good-humour. The working folk on a train, in their third or fourth classes, are always treated with indulgence and kindly consideration.

A Group of Russian Peasants.

I read the following in the *Statist* last year, finding later that it was contributed by a friend of mine:—

"Government emigration offices are situated all over Russia in Europe. These supply would-be settlers in Siberia with information as to water supply, timber, fuel, distances from market, etc. Intending settlers choose some of their number, at the expense of the government, to inspect the different tracts of land parcelled out for settlement, and select areas considered suitable for the settlers. This may take a whole year, and the deputed settlers return and report to their fellows. A petition is then sent in to the government—say that 100 men want to go to such and such a place. Then the government marks on the map that this land has been apportioned to the applicants, and it is set aside for them accordingly. The land is given free up to 275 acres per head. Each man thus has his own land. He cannot sell it, and it cannot be mortgaged either, though he get into debt. The land is his as long as he cares to work it. For special purposes, horse and cattle breeding, the government now permits larger areas up to 10,000 acres to be acquired, and helps settlers in this connection by providing, for breeding purposes, thoroughbred stallions and Jersey bulls. The government send the settlers down passage free, and as the people are simply peasants, doctors and nurses are provided to look after them and treat them for sickness, etc. Further, the settlers are given in certain cases a sum up to £20 to reach their destination. They are allowed, carriage free, to take one cow, implements, and other goods for their purposes. The government gives them free timber for house building, though the settlers have to cut it themselves. Should the settlers be short of money or funds for buying horses, ploughs, etc., they can get a credit through the Land Bank up to £20, which they have to pay back in instalments spread over a long period."

Does not a government which thus develops its country and moves its working population in vast numbers from places where they are not doing well to other places where they may do better well deserve to be called "fatherly" in its care for their interests?

It is well known to those who have been watching Russia's progress that she has of late, and especially last year, been drawing upon her enormous revenues and taking advantage of her unexampled prosperity, as one of the best-informed journalists in Europe[10] has stated, "for public works, railways, and canals, factories, schools, post offices, model farms and reform measures for the improvement of the lot of the working man." It was in the interests of her working poor that one of the most costly and far-reaching experiments ever undertaken by a government, at great financial sacrifice to itself, was launched just before war was declared—the legislation concerning *vodka*.

It surely is an inspiring thought that we and our new friend may tread the path of social reform together just when it has become alike the need and opportunity of our time! There is nothing so certain than that it is along this path that our two sovereigns will gladly lead us. We in our country have never before had King and Queen visiting the manufacturing districts of their realm, acquainting themselves with every detail of daily work, going simply and naturally into homes, and sharing the humble fare of the working classes. We have never had a king before—without reflecting upon any who have preceded him we may say it—who has gone amongst his soldiers and sailors, as one of themselves, crossing over to the front that he might see how they did, and show them that he was determined to know for himself the conditions under which they were so nobly doing their duty, so that they should not only have his leadership but all the sympathy he could give them.

It has been just the same in Russia. There, at last, has come the great departure from precedent and tradition for which the Emperor has always longed and felt to be possible since he came to London and said, "Some day it will be like that in Russia!" The "some day" has come at last. One felt it when he went into the Duma last year at the outbreak of the war, and, on his own initiative alone, addressed its members informally on the task of serving their country together. Other things have followed in quick succession! The Empress and her daughters became nurses at once as soon as the wounded soldiers began to be brought in. They wore the uniform, and were addressed as Sister Olga or Sister Tatiana like every one else, although the Russian Court has been held to be the most exacting and punctilious court in Europe. Again and again the Emperor has been to the front, endearing himself to his soldiers, to whom it is known that he equipped himself in a common soldier's uniform, before he passed it, with kit, rifle, and boots complete, and tramped miles across the country that he might know what it was like to be on the march.

Does it make no difference to Ivan Ivanoff to say to himself on the march when he thinks of his Emperor, "He knows what it's like, for he's done it himself? Somewhere he's thinking about his soldiers, and he *knows*." He was photographed in their uniform, just as one of themselves, and the photograph was distributed amongst the troops. "GOD save the Tsar!" is the one clamorous cry of the streets in Russia to-day, we are told. The Emperor and Empress show themselves in a balcony in Petrograd as naturally as King George and Queen Mary show themselves at Buckingham Palace when the crowd ask for them.

Such a thing has never been seen, or even thought of, before in Russia. The last time the Emperor came up from the Crimea to the capital, there were soldiers within speaking distance of each other along the entire length of rail, keeping watch and guard. Soon he will go about unattended, and without escort; and as it was with Queen Victoria, so "it will be like that in Russia."

Again, I want to dwell upon this link between us, and its tremendous promise for the future. The two greatest rulers in the world, closely and affectionately related, have the same ideals of what rulers should be, and want nothing better than to lead and serve their people; and GOD, in His providence, has given them at the same time both the power and opportunity for doing this splendid work together.

Never, probably, has the monarchical principle, in its best aspect, been so intelligently accepted in both empires as now. A near relation of the Emperor's, though much his senior, was telling me once of a recent visit he had paid to England, and of some of his experiences in the East End, where, under the guidance of a detective, he had visited some of the worst haunts.

"And do you know, bishop?" he said, "I learnt from that detective that everybody in London showed their respect for King Edward, at his death, by going into mourning; and the very thieves *stole* black to mourn him with the rest! There's the monarchical principle, going down even to the lowest classes in the nation!"

"But, sir," I ventured, "I don't think that men of that class would be thinking of him as a ruler, but as a sportsman."

"No! no!" he maintained. "It was the monarchical principle going down to the very lowest of the people!" And I am sure he thinks so, and tells the story to enforce it.

There can be no doubt that the monarchical principle, as we understand it, makes rapid progress in Russia. The Emperor has always been an autocrat, but his worst enemy could not accuse him of ever having been merely despotic; and surely, though gradually, he will be less and less an autocrat, and more and more constitutional in his rule. He meets the needs and satisfies the ideals of his people, as he embodies in his person government and rule. If any one thinks that Russia has a seething revolutionary spirit longing for expression and an outlet, I can't help feeling that they are utterly and entirely mistaken. Serious discontent and unrest prevail; but, as I will try and show later, it is directed against the social order rather than against the Emperor himself. Plots to kill him have been plots to overturn the social order, and nothing more.

Even political exiles in Siberia never blame him for their condition, as Mr. de Windt tells us: "I never once heard members of the imperial family spoken of with the slightest animosity or disrespect; and once when the Emperor was mentioned one of the exiles burst out with a bitter laugh—

"'The Emperor! You may be quite sure the Emperor does not know what goes on, or we should not be here a day longer.'"

The people are wholly loyal, and regard their ruler as embodying a government which is in their own interests as being his children. There can be no doubt that this is the feeling throughout the empire, however difficult it may be for some classes in our community to believe it.

For instance, as it has been pointed out,[11] "When not long ago in the House of Commons it was debated whether or no the King should pay a visit to the Emperor of Russia, and some one suggested that were the visit to be cancelled the immense majority of the Russian people would regard it as an insult, and that the Russian peasants bore no ill-will towards the Emperor, but rather complained of the results of a system of government which in the last few years has undergone, and is still undergoing, radical change." When such arguments were brought forward some of the Labour Members nearly burst with ironical cheers. Here, they thought, was the voice of officialdom, Torydom, and hypocrisy speaking. Now turn to the facts. When Professor Kovolievski was elected a member of the first Duma in the government of Karkov as an advanced Liberal Member, he, after his election, asked some of his peasant electors whether he was not right in supposing that had he said anything offensive with regard to the Emperor at his meetings there would have been no applause.

"'We should not only have not applauded,' was the answer, 'but we should have beaten you to death.'"

There is nothing of the merely sentimental in this feeling that their government is, and ought to be, paternal in its character. Every Russian peasant drinks it in from the first, for he gets his training in the *Mir* of his native village. It is there he learns what family and social rule really mean, and they are identical. His home is ruled by his father, the village by the elder; and everything is as constitutional and as democratic as it can be, or is anywhere else in the world. The children have their rights, but look up to and obey their father. They are free and responsible in village life, but yield to their elders. It is natural, therefore, and no other view is even possible, for men brought up in such surroundings to look outside the village and regard the State as a whole in the same way. There too they feel that they have full rights, and yet are under a firm, unquestioned, and paternal rule—the rule of him who, while rightly called their Emperor, yet is better known to themselves and loyally loved as their "Little Father."

FOOTNOTES:

[10] Dr. E. J. Dillon.

[11] The Hon. Maurice Baring.

CHAPTER VIII
THE STEPPES

Amongst all the interesting experiences of an unusually varied and adventurous life, since, in the very middle of my Oxford course I had, for health's sake, to spend a couple of years ranching in the River Plate, my long drives across the steppes stand out in bold and pleasing relief.

They were necessitated by a Mining Camp Mission in Siberia, for the steppes form a large part of the eastern portion of the Russian Empire, and do not belong to Russia proper at all, lying beyond the Volga and the Urals. It is in that part of Asiatic Russia that the development of the empire's vast resources is taking place with special rapidity, and our own countrymen are bearing a hand in it and playing no unworthy part.

I believe the word "steppes" is given to that undulating but level country in the provinces of Ufa and Orenburg, about two days' and two nights' journey by train east of Moscow, inhabited by the Bashkirs, the descendants of those Tartar hordes who nearly overwhelmed Russia at one time, and possibly Europe itself, and were called for their relentless cruelty "the Scourge of GOD."

Consecration of Burial Ground in the Siberian Steppes.

They are a fierce-looking race, even now, though peaceable enough, and it seems strange to find them so near to Moscow still, and to see them at their devotions when driving past their mosques on a Friday. They are great agriculturists, and a delightful sight is presented by their vast tracts of tender green wheat and oats shooting up as soon as the winter is over, and even while, in out-of-the-way hollows, snow still remains. The earth is black and very rich in character, and the seed, sown often before the end of September, lies nearly seven months under the protecting and fertilizing snow. As soon as this has gone and spring comes, the young crops shoot up with amazing speed and strength. Late frosts are terrible disasters, of course, under such circumstances.

But the *real* steppes, which resemble the veldt of Africa, or the pampas of South, and the prairie of North America, are those vast level plains, partly agricultural, partly pasture, and partly scrub and sand, which lie another day and night still further east, and extend for thousands of miles to the south till they reach nearly to the borders of Turkestan. These are the steppes I know best. There is also a pastoral steppe of large extent and of agricultural character just above the Black Sea.

If the reader will refer to the map he will see what a huge portion even of the great country of Siberia is taken up by the Kirghiz Steppes, and as they are extraordinarily rich in minerals, so far as one can judge from enterprises already successfully started, produce large crops, and sustain innumerable flocks and herds, it will be seen how much they are likely to count for in the progress of Russia. The Kirghiz, familiarly called the "Ks" in the mining camps, are a Tartar race, like the Bashkirs, and, like them also in religion, are Mohammedans; but while I saw mosques amongst the Bashkirs filled with praying congregations, I never saw either mosque or prayers amongst the Kirghiz, nor their women veiled. They are small in stature, very strongly built, rather like the Japanese, and splendid horsemen. A Kirghiz when mounted seems part of his horse as he dashes across the steppes at full speed with the merest apology for reins and bit, ready to pull up in the twinkling of an eye.

They struck me always as very friendly, though I have read that others have not found them so.

That they are very hospitable every one admits. A traveller, it is said, can go thousands of miles across the steppes without a rouble in his pocket, and want for nothing. Everywhere he will be hospitably entertained. A Russian, of course, asks nothing better than to have a guest, and considers himself honoured in being asked to take him in for a meal or for the night; and the Kirghiz are Eastern in their reception of guests as well.

In the steppes governments of Ufa, Orenburg, and Akmolinsk the population must be nearly seven millions, of which the great majority are the nomadic Kirghiz, living in tents in the summer, and taking their flocks and herds away to the south and into villages, where they can have roofs and walls during the seven months—at least!—of terrible winter.

The tent is a most comfortable abode, though not much to look at from outside. It has a wooden floor, with a rug or skins upon it, is circular in its area, but has no pole of any kind, being built up very neatly and ingeniously upon a framework of canes and laths until it is in shape like a well-spread-out low and evenly-rounded haystack. It has a movable top in its centre, which affords ample ventilation. Inside it is lined with felt, which has often prettily embroidered draperies fastened upon it; and outside the canework it is well covered over with stout canvas securely lashed into its place. It will be seen that no obstacle is presented to the strong winds which continually blow over the steppes, as there are no "corners" such as are spoken of in Job i. 14, which shows us that tents were raised upon four poles in early Israelitish days as they are still amongst the Bedouin tribes of North Africa and Arabia.

The beautifully and symmetrically rounded *uerta*, as the Kirghiz tent is called, receives every wind that sweeps over it, and never makes the slightest movement. At least twenty people could be, and often are, gathered inside when some festivity is afoot, though each family as a rule has its own tent. They are extremely attractive, and when I once went to see an American family, engaged in preliminary mining work, I found them with one of these tents for their living-room, set up with sideboard, dining-table, easy-chairs, etc., and another opposite to it fitted up as a most comfortable bedroom with brass beds and all the usual furniture, the little cookhouse also being not far away. Breathing in the marvellous air of the steppes, I thought I had never seen the "simple life" presented in a more alluring form. I have longed, indeed, ever since to have a month of it some time, and get as close to Mother Nature as it is possible to do in these busy days.

Outside a Kirghiz Uerta.

The descendants of Jonadab knew what they were about, and what was good for them, when they determined to keep to their pastoral life, and hold on to all their tent-dwelling traditions; and as for wine, no one need ever feel the need of such a stimulant in the invigorating air of those great plains.

Amongst the Kirghiz one feels an extraordinarily biblical atmosphere, and is back again in the days of Abraham and the patriarchs, and the "women in the tent," of whom Jael sang after the great victory. The men are attired much as Isaac and Ishmael, and Jacob and Esau were, and the women very probably keep the traditions of thousands of years in wearing their pretty nun-like head-dresses of white, which leave their pleasant faces free and uncovered.

These Kirghiz hardly ever use money. They grow "rich in many flocks and herds," and if they sold would immediately buy again. Some of them, however, are very well off, and I was told that one, who lived simply with his wife in a *uerta* on the steppes, had sent his only son to complete his education in Paris, and get a medical degree at its University. For this he would have to sell off some of the increase of his flock, and send the proceeds to his son.

Let me now explain how I came to be amongst these tent-dwelling folk at all. During my first visit to Petrograd I was asked one evening by a member of the Russia Company if I could appoint a chaplain to go out to Siberia once a year or so, and visit the scattered little groups of our own countrymen who are there, but, at that time, had never seen a clergyman nor had a service since coming into the country.

"There are unbaptized," he said, "and unconfirmed, and even those who need to be married with the service of their Church, who through no fault of their own, but through circumstances, have had to go without it. There are people who have been in Siberia all their lives, and some who have been there forty and fifty years, and never once had any ministration of their Church. Can nothing be done?"

This, of course, was a strong and direct appeal, and, after considering for a short time, it seemed impossible to appoint a chaplain for work of which one knew nothing, and so I proposed to go myself, which I found later was what it was hoped and expected that I should do. Accordingly in 1912 and again in 1913 I carried out this intention, and found that it practically took the form of a Mining Camp Mission; for, though I visited one or two other British communities, yet the most interesting part of both years' experiences was in going to the mines situated, except in one case, in the very heart of the steppes. Each, though employing thousands of Kirghiz and Russians, is managed by a British staff of between twenty and thirty, and is the property of a British company with its board of directors meeting in its offices in London.

I will describe two of these journeys, for without knowing something of the steppes and of those who live there, and indeed taking in something of their spirit, it is impossible to feel that one really knows Russia.

Four days and nights from Moscow brings one to Petropavlosk (Peter and Paul's town), and it is from there, in a southerly direction at first, and then heading towards the east, that the great Spassky Copper Mine is reached, for which a drive of a thousand miles, there and back, is necessary. I had not realized till just before I set out that I should have to drive on day and night without stopping for anything but food and to change horses, as there were no Russian rest-houses on that route, and the Kirghiz tents were impossible owing to the great number of living beings, other than human, which inhabited them. It was no light thing to undertake, as it meant leaving on Tuesday and getting in late on Saturday evening, and this only if all went well. Some people can sleep under such conditions during the night. I don't know how they possibly can, for there are no roads in any true sense of the word, and none of the vehicles which cross them have springs.

The manager of the mine had kindly sent down the usual *tarantass*, which, hooded like a victoria, is a very stout cart, lashed securely upon poles, and drawn by three horses or *troika*. There is no seat inside, but hay is placed over the bottom, and pillows and cushions on the top, and there one reclines during the day, and lies down at night. It all sounds very comfortable and even luxurious, but as there are no roads, and only the roughest of tracks with fearful ruts and soft places where water lingers, with sometimes a sloping bank down to a stream, and, as the wild driver keeps his horses at their full speed, one is hurled violently and roughly about the whole time, sleep, for me at least, is beyond my wildest hopes from start to finish.

Tarantass with its Troika for the Steppes.

For the first day or so I had the greatest difficulty to avoid biting my tongue in two as I was thrown about and it came between my teeth, and I used to look with amazement and envy at my Kirghiz conductor, on the box beside the driver, swaying about in all directions like a tree in a hurricane, but sound asleep. His name was Mamajam, and on our arrival he brought his little daughter Fatima to see me, and another youth named Abdullah, completing the Arabian Nights impression he had already given me.

There is no regularity in the arrangements for changing horses along the steppes. Sometimes one would drive about twenty *versts* (twelve and a half miles) and then change, while at others we would go on as far as sixty, or even eighty, *versts* (fifty miles) without any change at all. The horses are very strong and hardy, and are never allowed either food or drink until the journey is over; and, with the horses, the driver is changed also, as every man brings and understands his own. It was a wonderful study in character, temperament, and dress, for the men were extraordinarily different from each other, though all most attractive and interesting; the Kirghiz more so than the one or two Russians we had.

We carried our food, chiefly tinned, with us, but there was an abundance of eggs, butter, and white bread always to be got, and, most welcome sight, always the steaming *samovar*, with its promise of cheering and comforting tea. It is astonishing how one's ordinary food can be cut down in quantity when necessary. We gradually came down to two meals a day, and on the return journey these only consisted of eggs, bread and butter, and tea; and yet the simple life and magnificent air made one feel always extraordinarily fit and well and in good spirits.

The steppes, though vast solitudes as far as human habitations are concerned, are full of life and movement, and the most is made of the short summer. Caravans are continually meeting the traveller as he goes south or north, or crossing his route from east to west, or west to east, carrying tea from China, timber and other articles of commerce, travellers from town to town, or from one village to another, or a little band of colonists seeking land upon which to settle, or herdsmen in charge of sheep, oxen, or horses. Perhaps one's driver catches sight of another *troika* going in the same direction, and with a shrill cry urges on his team; the other, nothing loath, joins in, and for a quarter of an hour there is a most thrilling race. There is never a dull moment night or day, though perhaps the most inspiring times are those when one has just changed horses, and has a wild young Kirghiz on the box who, seeing an opportunity of showing off, stands up whirling his whip and, shrieking, yelling, whistling, like a demon, urges his horses to their utmost speed, making the dust and earth fly in all directions. It makes one feel that it is good to be alive.

The air is most transporting at that height, four thousand feet above sea-level; the whole steppes in the early summer are strewn with flowers, larks are singing overhead, streams are flowing on every side, there is a clear horizon as at sea, though now and then there is hilly ground, the sky is ever delightfully blue and without a cloud, and the sun shines brightly, though not too fiercely, from morn till eve. Nothing could be more delightful than that first experience, especially as one thought of the object of one's journey and the services of the coming Sunday. Then the wonderful nights, beginning with the sweet, bell-like sounds of the innumerable frogs after the birds had ceased. As I did not sleep I saw and enjoyed all that the nights had to give, and we had the full moon. First the golden sunlight gradually died away and the silvery light of the moon appeared, that in its turn, after what seemed an extraordinarily short time, giving place to the dawn, which shows itself sometimes more than an hour before the actual sunrise. Night on the steppes, like the day, is also full of movement, for many of those who travel long distances prefer to let their horses and bullocks feed and rest during the long day, when they enjoy their pasture best, getting their own rest also at the same time, basking in the sun, and continuing their journey through the night, which is never really dark.

My second night out, just after midnight, I was startled at seeing a camel come into view in the moonlight on my right, going in the opposite direction and dragging a small cart, but making no sound upon the grass. It looked quite spectral in the moonlight, and was followed by another, and yet another; then came a bullock, then a horse or two, one after another, then more camels, all with carts and in single file. Not a sound could be heard, and only at intervals men walked beside them. It went on and on, the strange, silent procession, and I could not think what manner of caravan it could possibly be. All the carts were small, carefully covered over, and evidently had small loads, though requiring powerful creatures to draw them; and then all at once I understood. It was smelted copper being taken down to the railhead from which I had come, and from the mine to which I was going! I then began to count how many had still to pass me, and reckoned up a hundred and six, so that there must have been nearly three hundred in all. They take three months to go down, load up with stores, and return, and yet I was told that such transport was cheaper than sending by rail will be when that part of the government of Akmolinsk is connected with the great Trans-Siberian line running from Petropavlosk both to Moscow and Petrograd.

Another time I should take the opportunity afforded by a pause when changing horses in the night to get a few hours' sleep in the *tarantass* in the open air, which would, of course, make all the difference, and which would then be quite possible. But if I had done it on this occasion I should have had to lose a Sunday instead of arriving on the Saturday evening. I was well repaid, for though nothing more than a notice was sent quickly round, "The bishop has come, and there will be services at the manager's house to-morrow at half-past ten and at six, and Holy Communion at half-past seven," yet at half-past seven every one of our countrymen was there and received Communion except the wife of one member of the staff ill in bed. The manager's two little boys were there to be present at the first early Anglican celebration of Holy Communion ever taken beyond the Urals. A beautiful *ikon*, flowers, and two lights adorned the temporary altar. Others than our own countrymen attended the other services. It was a glorious day to have, including as it did attendance at the Russian Church in the morning when our own service was over.

This great mining property includes Karagandy, where the coal is, and to which I came first; Spassky, where the smelting-works had been set up, some forty miles further on; and Uspensky, where the mine itself is, some fifty miles further still. From Spassky I went to Uspensky by motor-car, and spent three days there with the foreman of the mine and his family. I went down the mine also to make acquaintance with the Kirghiz who are at work there, and knocked off for myself some specimens of the rich ore.

The foreman and his family—two girls and two sons of between twenty and thirty—had been in New Zealand, in the Backs, and it was no new thing for them to have a bishop stay and give them services. The wife was a particularly good and devout woman, and in all the years she had been there had never once had the happiness of attending a service of her own Church. The two young men were shy fellows, but the manager having first prepared the way, I took them in hand, and, finding they were ready to come to a decision in life, instructed and confirmed them. On these missions, as with Philip and the eunuch, we cannot lose such opportunities; and I shall not forget the Celebration, early on the day I left, when that whole family received Communion together. I know what a joy, such as she had never expected, it was to that good woman thus to have family unity; and, as she died suddenly before the year was over, I shall always feel that my long journey across the steppes was fully worth while if it were only for the happiness it had brought her in enabling her for once in her life to receive Communion with all the members of her family.

I had another most interesting experience before leaving Spassky and the Akmolinsk Steppes. Some little time before my arrival, two of the staff had lost their lives in the smelting-works and been buried in a little plot of ground with two monuments placed above them. One of the memorials was of pure copper, the other of stone, and there was a wooden railing round the small enclosure. The manager asked me to consecrate this little plot of ground with a larger space added to it, so that they might have their own little GOD'S acre.

As soon as the Russian priest heard that this was to be done he immediately asked if he and his people might be present and share in the service? And to this, of course, we readily agreed. It was impossible, however, to draw up any joint service, as we were ignorant of each other's language, so I arranged that he should say a few prayers first and that I should take our own service afterwards. This he was very glad to do, and, robed in his vestments as for the Liturgy, he prayed for the departed, singing with his people, present in great numbers, a touching little litany, and finishing with the offering of incense. As I looked at all those fellow Christians of ours and their priest, and then outside at the great circle of the vast steppes stretching away in all directions, so suggestive of greatness of spirit, I felt most deeply moved as I took the censer from him and, offering the incense as he had done, led the way, censing the boundaries of the new burial-ground marked out by stones. Our little community followed singing, "O GOD, our help in ages past," every line of which helped us all to realize a little at least of that large-hearted view of life and of death which no other passage of Scripture gives us with the directness and grandeur of Psalm xc.

The people looked on at this simple little procession with the closest attention and sympathy, and then, after an address—an entirely new experience for them in a religious service—I proceeded to the consecration of the ground. I should fancy it is the only instance, as yet, of clergy of the two Churches actually sharing a service together; and that was especially in my mind as I took the good priest's censer to offer, just as he had done and from the same censer, "an oblation with great gladness," feeling to the full "how good and joyful it is for brethren to dwell together in unity." I should say of that service also that it was quite worth while taking that long journey across the steppes to have it.

The prevailing idea of Siberia in this country is, as we all know, that it is a terrible waste of ice and snow, a land of mines and of convicts, ravaged by packs of wolves; and this is not at all an incorrect impression of the greater part of it and for the longest period of the year. All that is wrong in the impression is that it leaves out the five months of the year in which there is the glow and charm of the tropics, with growth and upspringing life and beauty on every hand. The steppes are a paradise of singing birds and blooming flowers and flowing streams, where the air is joyous to breathe, invigorating, quickening, and inspiriting beyond description. These are the Siberian Steppes I have known and traversed and loved, and long and hope to see again.

But I am keenly alive to all the real and ever-present sense of peril which the winter brings with it as soon as it comes, and which it keeps steadily before the mind till it is over for all who have to meet it and struggle against it. I have heard men speak of the terrible blizzards and the appalling cold; of the deadly gloom, when the air is so full of snow that they can hardly see a hand before their faces, and they wander uncertainly for a whole day and night together until they give themselves up for lost, to find after all, when the storm is over, that they are only a few yards away from their own doors, or in the middle of the street from which they had started.

They instantly drop their voices on the Kirghiz Steppes when they begin to speak of winter, and on some faces there comes at once that beaten look which, whenever it appears, is testimony that the man has measured himself against the sterner forces of Nature or of human life, and has failed.

Inside a Kirghiz Uerta.

Tolstoi's *Master and Man* gives a very clear and convincing account of what a snowstorm may mean for even experienced travellers. There the scene is laid in Russia, and between one village and another in a country often traversed; but the vast spaces of Siberia in that long, gloomy winter must be specially fraught with dangers and terrors during those swiftly rising and deadly *boirams*, as the wind-storms are called, which completely obliterate all landmarks while they last, and which are not to be met with anywhere else in the inhabited parts of the world. At Spassky they told me of a Kirghiz horseman who had been found one morning, during the preceding winter, just outside his home, horse and rider rigid in the snow and frozen stiff, both of them dead for hours. They had struggled against the *boiram* as long as they could, the man probably urging on his horse to the last, and both giving up the struggle together as the awful frost took possession of them, so swiftly that there was no falling off for the one nor sinking down for the other. And, if they had only known it, or the blinding storm had permitted them to see, they were at the very door of their home and within reach of warmth and food and shelter.

I remember once saying to friends that I supposed when travelling in winter they could make themselves very comfortable by packing themselves in with "hot-water foot-warmers." "Hot-water foot-warmers!" they exclaimed. "Why, the frost would have them and destroy them completely almost before we had left the door."

Then the wolves are there also! Siberia has not changed in that respect from the weird land of which we have read as long as we can remember, and is still the haunt of the most fierce and untiring enemies which man and beast alike have to fear when they are the hunters and not the hunted. The fair

Siberia of the glorious summer knows no wolves. Then there is food enough and to spare always within reach, and there are homes and family life even for wolves to think of and be happy about. There is no need then, though they are gregarious by nature, for them to join together. Each can fend for himself, and have enough for all his family and to spare. Not a wolf is to be seen except very rarely, and the traveller never even thinks of them with fear as, singly, sleek, and well fed, they slink away immediately as soon as seen. It is altogether different when winter comes, and hunger, even famine, gets a grip upon them because so many other creatures are hibernating. Then the quarry must be of different character, and nothing is too strong or big for a huge pack well led. Once they have been driven by stern necessity to combine together and choose their leader they will stick at nothing and attempt almost anything.

A friend of mine, born in Petrograd, tells us of an old travelling carriage of his father's, in which he and his brothers and sisters, when children, used to play.

"It was raised very high from the ground," he says, "only to be reached by a small ladder, so as to be out of the reach of wolves."

Just the same stories are told after every winter as those of which we have so often read in prose and verse; and, out of the many told me as happening quite recently, I select the following:—

Three winters ago a wedding party went from their village, in the Altai, where the ceremony had taken place in the morning at the home of the bride, to the village where the bridegroom lived, and to which he was now taking back his newly-wedded wife. They were a hundred and twenty in number, and made a large party, with their horses and sledges, and were not afraid; but an unusually large pack of wolves was out that afternoon, and, soon scenting them, gave chase. Party after party were overtaken, pulled down, and, with horses as well, devoured. The bride and bridegroom and best man were in the front sledge with good horses, and kept ahead till they were quite close to the village, when they too were overtaken by a few of the strongest and swiftest of their pursuers. To save themselves the bridegroom and best man threw out the bride, and thus stopped the pursuit for a time sufficiently for them to gain the village. It was a shocking thing to do, but when the villagers began to question and help them out the awful explanation was forthcoming! The two men had gone mad with fright, and had not known what they were really doing. In that terrible hunting down, with the shrieks and despairing cries of their friends, as they were overtaken, ever ringing in their ears as they urged their own terror-stricken horses forward, it is little wonder that their minds gave way.

Let there be no mistake, therefore, about the steppes. The reader may keep the new impression (if it is new) that I have endeavoured to give of a most beautiful, rich, and fertile country; and which I am hoping to be visiting again while this book is being read, finding, I hope, this country of the wolves story rejoicing in all the glow and beauty of summer. But still, for nearly seven months of the year, that Siberia is the old Siberia still, fast bound in the grip of an appalling frost, waging, in its storms, a never-ceasing battle against human enterprise and effort; and the haunt of those insatiable and savage creatures which seem to stand out from all other creatures in being devoid, when in packs, of all fear or dread of man.

The steppes above Turkestan, which I visited last, are milder in climate than those of Akmolinsk. Great parts of them are sand, with a sage-like scrub, dear to the heart of camels; and they have a drier and even more invigorating air than that of the northern plains. Across these I travelled my five hundred miles in a Panhard motor-car, with a wild Russian chauffeur who knew no fear. He dashed across a country which practically had no roads and resembled a rough Scotch moor, with an *élan* that the most daring French chauffeur might envy. He was a fine fellow, Boroff by name, and carried me on as before, day and night, and again with sunshine for the one and moonlight for the other. "The devil's wagon" is the name the wondering Kirghiz have given the motor-car from the first, but it is the last description it deserves. My journey of under twenty-four hours from the railhead to the Atbazar Mining Camp, if I had had to go by camel, as I expected might be possible until my actual arrival, would have taken me some twelve days, or even more.

All the transport in these steppes is by camels, and I could not be satisfied until I had made a small expedition upon one, and shall, perhaps, have to do the same again; but modern appliances are not to be despised, and no one can wish for a better experience of the steppes than to make the journey in the middle of summer and in a good modern motor-car.

CHAPTER IX
RUSSIA'S PROBLEM

The Social Problem, as it presents itself to thoughtful people in Russia, really demands a book to itself. No doubt it will come before long, and from some experienced pen. It is only possible for me just to touch upon it in this chapter, which one must write; or else even this very general view of Russia's life of to-day would be utterly inadequate and incomplete. And, in so doing, I shall have to try and show how different it is in Russia from the same problem as presented in other countries in Europe.

It is well known, for instance, that the great question for ourselves waiting for solution at some early date is the social question. What was called for us the "Triple Alliance" in the world of labour, the Union of the Railway, Transport, and Mining Workers was completed just before war broke out; and, though with a patriotism beyond praise all needs and desires of their own are put aside for the present, our workers will give expression to their wishes at no distant day after peace comes. Even before this book is in print the masses in Germany, grimly silent so long except for the ever-increasing votes for their socialistic representatives, silent even during the disillusionment which has come to them these last six months, may have at last spoken out. We are told that their leader, Herr Bebel, who is said to have known the German character through and through, declared that the first serious defeat experienced by Germany "would produce a miracle." Social unrest is still universal.

Russian Service at the Atbazar Mine.

We find it, therefore, as we should expect to do, in Russia; and more general, perhaps, and more acute than at any other previous time, just before the war was declared. This, it may be remembered, is stated to have been one of the reasons why the curt and hurried ultimatum was presented at Petrograd, where it was thought that social troubles and dangers were so serious that it would be impossible for the government even to think of going to war. We have been told,[12] though it was probably not known outside Russia at that time, what a good turn Germany really did to the Russian government and the Russian people by turning their thoughts from their own grave difficulties to the dangers which threatened them from without. At that time, we are assured, not only Petrograd, but every big manufacturing district of Russia, was shaking with revolt of a peculiar kind, and civil war on the point of breaking out. In Petrograd there were barricades already erected, at least 120,000 were on strike, tramcars had been broken up, attacks upon the police had taken place, factories were garrisoned in expectation of attack, the Cossacks were everywhere—openly in the streets, hidden away in places most threatened. The police arrested those who were supposed to be leaders, but it made no difference, for the people needed no leading. They were all so thoroughly in the movement. Indeed, we are told, "things seemed to the Russian government to be as bad as they could very well be; and orders were actually given for the severest possible repressive measures, which would, perhaps, have involved a large-scale battle, probably a massacre, and certainly a state of war in the capital." It would have been "Red Sunday" over again, only this time infinitely and more ominously worse. A great calamity was narrowly escaped.

Now there is this to be noticed about this Russian upheaval, and this social bitterness and discontent expressing itself in the way with which we are only too sadly familiar, and which claims our attention as being so entirely different from similar movements of our own. The Russian workers made no demands, had no special grievances nor complaints which they wished to make known. In all strikes one has previously heard of there has been some hardship or injustice to bring forward, some claim or request to urge. Here there was nothing of the kind. "They were not on strike," we are told, "for higher wages. In no single case did the men make a demand from their masters. In no single case had a man gone on strike because of a grievance which his master could put right. No concessions by the masters could have brought the men back to work. The only answer they returned when asked why there was a strike was that they were dissatisfied with their lives, and that they intended to disorganize the State until these things were altered." It is clear, therefore, that the social unrest, and the activity which has so long resulted from it, have not a very definite aim as yet. Hence the Nihilist. He is dissatisfied, embittered, smarting under a sense of wrong; and while he does not see how he can put things right, feels that he must do something, and so destroys. "That at least will be something," he feels, "then we can begin again."

This, we can further see, will be the youthful *student's* view if dissatisfied and discontented, and without either experience or constructive and practical knowledge to suggest how the wrong may be put right. Some of us, therefore, think that Russia's greatest social danger arises from the *student* part of her population, and that her great problem—a vital one for her to solve, and soon—is how to deal fairly and wisely with them, and, caring for them as paternally as she does for her peasant population, incorporate them fully and intimately into her national life.

It is from the educated classes that social unrest and discontent have proceeded in Russia, and from them that those agents have come who have spread wild and daring dreams of change and revolution amongst the working classes of the towns, and, although that has not been so successful, amongst the peasantry also.

To some extent their socialistic ideas have been echoes from Western Europe. I remember being told, when I first went to Petrograd, "We usually have your bad weather here about eight or ten days after you, only we have it worse." It would seem that the rule holds good in other ways also, for Sir Donald Mackenzie Wallace tells us, in one of his three deeply interesting chapters on social difficulties in Russia, that during the last two centuries all the important intellectual movements in Western Europe have been reflected in Russia, and that these reflections have generally been what may fairly be called exaggerated and distorted reflections of the earlier socialistic movements of the West, but with local peculiarities and local colouring which deserve attention.

He goes on to explain how the educated classes, absorbing these ideas from abroad, just as ideas, and not as relating to the conditions of life in Russia as closely as in England, France, and Germany, from which they came, have quite naturally been less practical in the conclusions they have drawn from them, if indeed they have pushed their ideas to any conclusion at all. We are shown plainly by this lucid and well-informed writer how natural it has been for Western Socialists to be constructive and definite in their aims, while Russians could only be destructive. Nihilism is made clear, and we understand its origin, while we can equally well understand what we are so reassuringly told about its present decline. This does not imply necessarily that Russian thinkers and workers are becoming less socialistic in sympathy and aims, but more practical; and that they are learning, just as the West has taught them, that the only way in which they can hope to advance their own views is to use all the legal means which their government, as it becomes ever more democratic and constitutional, will increasingly give them.

But amongst all the different classes who may be called educated, the university students of both sexes form the class which most claims our sympathies, and constitutes, I consider, Russia's gravest problem. There are ten universities in the empire, only one of which contains less than 1,300 students, while the leading ones far exceed this number—Moscow having just under 10,000, and Petrograd about 8,500. We can hardly realize what such numbers mean for the national life, when over 40,000 men and women are receiving university education and being prepared for professional careers. Over 15,000 are studying law, nearly 10,000 are receiving a scientific education before taking up work as chemists, engineers, etc., another 10,000 are studying medicine, comparatively few only being left for the teaching profession. There are only about a hundred divinity students.

In addition to these there are Russian students in all the universities of Europe. I have never been able to ascertain their actual numbers, but at Geneva, Lausanne, Berne, Leipzig, Berlin, and other great centres of education I have always been told, not only that they were there in no small numbers, but that they were the keenest and most attentive of all the students in the class, the first to come, and the last to leave, always in the front seats, and unflagging in their attention. They are evidently most eager to learn, and are turned out from all the universities of Europe and from their own, extremely well equipped and prepared for professional work. Then a vast number of students of this class are pitiably poor, straining every nerve, putting up with privations undreamed of elsewhere, in order to get through the preparation for their life's work.

Many of them, great numbers of them indeed, must be miserably disappointed. Town and city life, upon which the professional classes must rely chiefly in seeking the means of gaining their livelihood, has not developed as yet in proportion to that of the agricultural population; and certainly at nothing like the rate which would be necessary if all those educated and trained at the universities were to be provided with careers and given an adequate opportunity. The supply is far, far greater than the demand.

Thus we have in Russia a large class of really competent, brainy, well qualified young graduates of both sexes, naturally longing to take their part in the life, work, and affairs of their country, urged on also by their poverty to seek and even demand it; and yet many, it seems to me sometimes that it must be far the greater number, must be unable to find it. Here obviously are all the materials for a real social danger; and students, therefore, always appear in stories of plots and conspiracies, always fill an important place in plays of the same kind, and are always to the fore in tumults and demonstrations. It must be so, for they are the one really embittered class, and to them it must seem sometimes that there can be no hope for them at all in the social order as it is, and that its only possibility for them lies in its being destroyed and reconstructed.

A Class of Russian Students with their Teachers.

In many of our centres of work abroad we have a *foyer* where the foreign students can meet, and at Geneva last year with great difficulty we had opened a hostel for Russian students when the war broke out. There one heard the most touching stories of their poverty, and yet of their pride and independence, and also of the special temptations to which their poverty exposed them. Some landlords, for instance, are not slow to tell girls that they would live better and more cheaply if they would temporarily "keep house" with one of the young men students, and occupy one room! Our hostel was hurried on last year as we heard of many instances of this kind, and a generous friend in Petrograd helped me very largely in finding the money. Everything was to be supplied at cost price, and no profits were to be made, the two English ladies in charge giving their services. There was a restaurant also which supplied good food at very moderate rates, and how moderate may be judged from the charge made for afternoon tea of a halfpenny! It consisted of a cup of tea and a small roll of bread without butter.

The first time I saw how cheaply the foreign students at Geneva lived was one festival evening when they invited me to supper, and when we had chicken salad with bread and butter followed by dessert, tea, and coffee, for which the charge was about fivepence each. The year after that I entertained them in return and gave them a Christmas party at which there were fourteen nationalities present, mainly Slav. Nothing could have been more interesting than that gathering, nor could any host have had more grateful guests. Last year the Noel Fest could not be held as there were no students; but I hope next Christmas may possibly see the war over, and that we may have a Slav evening party in Geneva once again.

It may be well to mention here how there comes to be a *foyer* or club for Russians and other students at Geneva. It is a part of the organization connected with the World Student Christian Federation, which had its beginning in the eighties in the United States of America, as a movement to promote an interest in missionary work amongst students. In 1887 a deputation came over to this country to tell the student world what was going on across the Atlantic, and the student foreign missionary union was the result. Next the Christian Student Movement extended itself into all our European countries, and finally the World's Federation was accomplished at Wadstena Castle in Sweden in 1895. It is directed by a committee consisting of two representatives from each national movement, with Mr. John R. Mott, so well known, as its general secretary. Its operations now extend into all the leading countries of the world. There is a biennial conference, and it is admitted that one of the most interesting of any yet held was the one at Constantinople in 1911, which was attended by patriarchs representing all the Orthodox Churches of the East. It is not an undenominational movement, but exactly the opposite—a call rather to all the Churches of the world to be consistent in their Christian profession and "walk worthy of the vocation wherewith they are called." It is not a society nor a religious body, but a movement or union, and its basis, to be accepted by all its voluntary members and officers, is the declaration, "I desire, in joining this Union, to declare my faith in JESUS CHRIST as my Saviour, my LORD, and my GOD." There is no reason why any Christian in the world should not join it. Roman Catholics, Orthodox, Anglicans, and members of other Churches the world over can have no possible difficulty in making such a simple declaration if there is any reality at all in their sense of membership in CHRIST'S Church; and there is every reason *why* a Christian student should join a movement which is the only one of its kind to aim at work for CHRIST in those places where it is most urgently and sorely needed, and where it is most likely to be truly fruitful—the universities and colleges of the world.

There we have to-day those who have to lead and guide and guard the course of the whole world to-morrow. It is in the universities of the world that some of those influences which are most hostile and inimical to true social well-being are first set in motion, and it is there most certainly that we must begin if we wish to see the world made better and won for GOD. The war has made us long, I hope, for better things in a way the world has never dreamt of before, because there has never been anything in all history which has so focussed attention for the watching world upon a simple and direct question of right and wrong. The issue is even more momentous and significant than that. This great question of righteousness and unrighteousness must be answered by every one in the world according to his belief or unbelief. It is just a question for us all to settle whether our own interests, individual or national, or our duty to GOD comes first. The issue has never been more simply stated, and the Church of CHRIST has never in all her history had such a magnificent opportunity of giving her message, and proclaiming her mission. I hope, therefore, that all my readers will take an early opportunity of learning all they can about the Christian Student Movement, and satisfy themselves as to its fitness for helping the whole Church of CHRIST to avail herself to the full of this GOD-given opportunity and possibility.

A *foyer* is a necessary centre for students wherever a branch of the movement has been formed, and it would be difficult to speak too warmly of its value for its members. I have mentioned this movement here, briefly enough, I fear, of necessity, because I should think there is no place where it is more needed, nor, as far as I can judge, more likely to continue to succeed, than in Russia. In Petrograd there are already a number of influential and wealthy Russians deeply interested in its work amongst the men students. They include a near relation of the Emperor, and the work is directed by a number of extremely competent and earnest Americans. I had an opportunity of meeting and addressing them when in Petrograd a year ago.

The work amongst the girl and women students is being carried forward very quietly by our own country-women, who are full of hope. But up to the present a great deal of caution and wisdom has had to be exercised, both because the authorities have so long been accustomed to look suspiciously at anything which seemed to promote associations amongst students, and because students themselves, for reasons already given, have naturally looked askance at anything which was obviously working in the direction of law and order. The movement, more and more, it will be seen, is one of the soundest of modern efforts in the direction of real social improvement, because it begins at the right end, with those who are thinking and pondering life's problems before launching out to try their best to solve them. Nowhere has it been more needed, as I have said, than in Russia, and nowhere has it made a better start. The hopeful thing about Russia just now is that *every one* is most keenly and profoundly interested in the social well-being of the people—on the one hand anxious to obtain it more fully for themselves, and on the other really wishful to give and promote it, even if watchful and cautious lest they should make mistakes and have to draw back.

And surely caution is very necessary in Russia. It is only a little over fifty years since the emancipation of the serfs. Let any one think of Russia with a servile population so short a time ago, and then think of what she is to-day, and they will form some idea of the extraordinary social improvement and transformation which has taken place. Yet with all this caution the desire to see improvement is general, and no one is satisfied with the lives of the working-classes in the large towns as they are. It is well known indeed, as I have already said, that Russia has been absorbed in plans for social improvement for the last few years, and was meaning to launch out into great undertakings this very year. Those plans are only deferred, we hope, and will be taken up with greater zest and confidence than ever when peace comes. Perhaps the delay will prove to have been an inestimable gain, if it has made it clearer than before that there are certain examples it might be well to avoid. A great deal has been said and written of late years of the vast superiority of German municipal government and organization, and certainly no cities in Europe approach those of Germany for attractiveness and excellence of arrangements as to streets, parks, public buildings, and imposing blocks of flats for private families of all classes. Germans have been for many years now animated by the very best spirit of municipal initiative and responsibility, and have shown a really worthy civic pride. Railway stations, post offices, walks, and squares in Germany are beyond comparison with those of any other country. And yet I am assured that much is sacrificed for effect and appearance; and I was astonished to hear, a little while ago, how miserably inadequate was the accommodation that even a skilled artisan in Berlin could afford to have.

A well-known social authority, Mr. T. C. Horsfall, writing in the *Spectator* last December, told us that there is terrible overcrowding in nearly all large German towns, and that the overcrowded tall blocks of buildings are themselves too closely crowded together, and the effect is bad both for health and morality. The death-rate, including that of infants, is much higher with them than with us. And I cannot help thinking that the effect of giving families only two rooms and a small scullery, one living-room and one bedroom for all, must have its effect upon the morality of a population. Whatever the cause, we are told that in Berlin 17 per cent. of the births are registered as illegitimate, in Munich as many as 28 per cent., in Vienna over 40 per cent., while in London they are only 5 per cent.

"The effect on German town populations," Mr. Horsfall states, "especially on the poorer inhabitants of Berlin, of the conditions existing in German towns is described in an appeal made in or about the year 1886 by Professor Schmoller to his fellow-countrymen to deal adequately and promptly with those conditions. The appeal has been reprinted in an important Report published in 1911 by Dr. Werner Hegemann:

> 'The circumstances are so terrible that one can only wonder that the consequences have not been even worse. Only because a large part of these poor people have brought from their earlier life a store of good habits, of religious tradition, of decent feeling, into these dens, has the worst not yet been reached. But the children and young people who are now growing up in these holes must necessarily lose the virtues of economy, domesticity, family life, and all regard for law and property, decency, and good habits. He

who has no proper dwelling, but only a sleeping-place, must fall a victim to the public-house and to drink.... The community to-day is forcing the lower strata of the factory proletariat of large towns by its dwelling conditions with absolute necessity to fall back to a level of barbarism and bestiality, of savagery and rowdiness, which our forefathers hundreds of years ago had left behind them. I maintain that there lies the greatest danger for our civilization.'"

With such examples as this before her we must trust that Russia will set about promoting the social well-being of her people with all her characteristic independence, and determine that in their housing she will have only those "great spaces" which are her characteristic features in so many other ways. We have to tread this same road of social reform also when the war is over, and it is good to think that we may, perhaps, be able to take it, just as we have carried on the war, without any party questions or party spirit connected with it, as will be the case also in Russia. It is even more inspiring to think, again let me say it, that we and our new friend may tread this path together: comparing notes and making plans together as we go. That would be indeed an *Entente* worth the name, when it was not in order that we might make war together, only that we had come to an agreement, but that we might help each other's peoples in all the arts of peace. Mr. Baring tells us that he was once drinking tea with a Russian landowner who calls himself a moderate liberal, and when, in their conversation, the Anglo-Russian agreement was mentioned, he exclaimed (and I have no doubt he expressed the feelings of many others who desire the social good of Russia as he did so), "This is the most sensible thing the Russian government has done for the last forty years!"

The English Church of S. Andrew, at Moscow, with the Parsonage.

FOOTNOTES:

[12] "Anglitchanin" in *The Contemporary Review*, Nov., 1914.

CHAPTER X
The Anglican Church in Russia

I welcome the opportunity that this chapter affords me of defining the position taken by our Church in Russia, for it is just the same there as in Germany, France, Belgium, and the other countries in our jurisdiction. Many English Churchmen deprecate, while others strongly resent, our having clergy, churches, and services on the Continent of Europe at all. They consider it an interference with the Church of the country, schismatical in its character, and a hindrance and impediment to the reunion of Christendom. Some English clergy come, therefore, into the jurisdiction of North and Central Europe from their own parishes, and though their own Church may have its services there, ostentatiously attend the services of the Roman Catholic Church. Young men coming out for business, girls taking positions as nurses and governesses, and others coming for health and enjoyment, are sometimes advised by their clergy not to go near the English Church, but to attend Mass and "worship with the people of the country."

What, I fancy, many of our brethren at home, clergy and laity alike, fail very often to realize is the great difference between a temporary and permanent residence abroad. Many of us know what it is to spend a holiday in some simple and beautiful village—in the Black Forest, for instance—amongst devout and good people, far away from one's own Church, and where it is just as natural as anything can be, and completes the friendly feeling between us, to go to church on Sunday and worship with them. Even in an unfamiliar service we have our own Prayer Books, and can read Collect, Epistle, and Holy Gospel, and be in spirit and touch with our brethren worshipping in their own churches all over the world.

There is something to be said, therefore, for sharing the worship of the people of the place when passing through or making but a short stay, though, even in holiday resorts or "Sports centres," the opportunities which our Church, chaplain, and services offer are too precious and important to be lost or undervalued. But there is nothing whatever to be said for leaving a community of our own countrymen, permanently resident in another land, without the ministrations of their own Church, if they can possibly be supplied to them; and still less if, as in Russia and some other places, the people can find the means of support themselves.

Will any of our brethren seriously maintain that, when families have to leave this country and go to live on the Continent of Europe, they must leave their own Church and be received into the Roman or Greek Communion? Or, if not, will they consider that they ought to frequent the services of those Churches as outsiders, never having the experiences and helps afforded by the sacramental means of grace? It must be one or the other. If abroad we are not to attend the services of our own Church, then the only alternative is either to leave it altogether or to live the maimed spiritual life of those who are without the ministry of the Word and Sacraments.

And, moreover, if it is thought that one of the pressing duties of our time is to follow our brethren across the ocean to Canada, though even there the Roman Church claims to be the "Church of the country" in its French-speaking territory, and to give them the ministrations of religion, why are we not to follow them across the Channel, when they leave their country for precisely the same reason, to extend its business and commercial influence and to serve its interests in diplomatic, consular, and professional life? To think at all carefully over the situation is to see at once that our people in North and Central Europe have just the same rights (and I don't ask for anything more than that) to the services of their own Church as anywhere else in the world.

Take, for instance, this typical case of a friend of mine living in one of the cities of Europe, and now retired from business, but still living on where he is so well known, and where he has many ways of making himself of use. He was married young, and his bride went with him to make her home abroad. They had their own Church there, and there they took their children to be baptized and, when old enough, to worship, be confirmed, and become communicants. There those children have been married, and from there gone out into the world to make new homes. In his house the clergy have been always made welcome, and have visited them when sick, counselled them when necessary, and received much valuable advice in return. Can any one be heartless enough, or foolish enough, to say that there ought to have been no English Church in that place at all, and that he and his young wife ought to have attended the Church of the country, and with their descendants been lost to their own?

Then there are girls at school, young men learning the language, governesses, nurses, lads in the training stables, girls dancing on the stage—these are well shepherded in Paris—and others. Are they to feel in after life, "Just at the critical time, when I needed it most, my Church was not there to give me the helping hand—and all might have been so different if it had been!" I will not dwell upon all the priceless opportunities afforded us abroad, where touch is more quickly gained, and more easily maintained, of winning during sickness and at other times those who have never been in touch with clergy or Church at home, bringing them out into the light, gaining them for the Church, and sending them home to "strengthen the brethren" there.

Most of our clergy, from Northern Russia to Southern France and the Pyrenees, have their inspiriting stories to tell of the services they have rendered to the Church at home in this way, and yet that Church, if some of our brethren could have their way, would disown them. It won't bear seriously thinking of, this objection to English Church work abroad; and surely it rings more true to what we feel is the Englishman's duty wherever he is, when we read that our countrymen, after settling at Archangel in the sixteenth century, built their warehouses and their Church at the same time, and wished, in their adopted country, to worship GOD "after the manner of their fathers."

I have taken a little time to explain our continental position thus, because it is the same in every country, is thoroughly understood, and never, as far as I know, resented. We always make it perfectly clear that we never wish to interfere with the Church of the country, nor the religion of its people, but are there to shepherd our own. And it is a curious thing that in Catholic Belgium, as it is called, with people devoted to their Church, and with a clerical government such as they have had for at least the last forty years, our Anglican clergy receive from the Belgian government the same recognition, status, stipends, grants for houses, etc., as are given to the clergy of the country.

But nowhere is the position of our Church more fully, sympathetically or affectionately recognized than in Russia. Nowhere would it be felt, as there, a grave and responsible neglect of duty on our part if we were to leave our own people without the ministrations of their own Church. They go further than this in sympathetic feeling, for they consider that there is a special link and bond of union between our Church and their own. An anonymous but evidently extremely well-informed writer about Russia, over the *nom de plume* of "Anglitchanin" in a leading Review[13] a month or two ago, said, in the course of his article on *Russia and the War*, "the English Church is said to be very like the Greek Orthodox. It is not so in fact, but in Russia it is believed to be so by *all classes of the population*. That is indeed the one thing about England that they all know. I have known more than one peasant ask me, 'Is England beyond Germany—far? or beyond Siberia? But your religion is like ours.'

"The origin of this belief," he adds, "is to be found in the fact that we are not Lutherans on the one side, and on the other do not acknowledge the Pope."

They welcome our bishops and clergy to their services in their robes, and attend ours in the same way. When the late Duke of Edinburgh married the daughter of the Emperor Alexander, the service took place first in the cathedral with the Russian rite, with Dean Stanley present in his robes, and then a second time in the English Church with our own service, with the Russian clergy present in the sanctuary. The Bishop of London also loves to describe his reception at the great Troitsky Monastery near Moscow, where he attended the services in cope and mitre, and with pastoral staff, and was greeted by all the clergy present as one of their own bishops; and the last time I heard him describe the beautiful ceremonial, he added significantly, "I should not have been received in that way at S. Peter's, Rome"; but who can say what may be the outcome of this war? There has been a wonderful drawing together of the French and English clergy, and perhaps we may soon have more brotherly relations with the Roman clergy, even though we do not have inter-communion.

When four of our English bishops went to Russia with a large party of Members of Parliament and business men, three years ago, the chaplain at Petrograd arranged a choral celebration of Holy Communion in his church, and it was attended by some of the highest dignitaries of the Russian Church, who were present in their robes and took part in the procession, following the service as closely and intelligently as they could. No clergy of our Church have ever gone to Russia to learn what they could for themselves, or give lectures, or act as members of deputations, and come into touch with the Orthodox clergy and been disappointed with their reception; but, on the contrary, they have often been quite astonished at the warmth of welcome offered them and the keen interest shown towards them.

I had no idea until I had read what the *Contemporary Review* has told us that there is nothing so well known about England, throughout *all classes* of the population, as the similarity of the two Churches and the religion they represent; but I can speak for the archbishops, bishops, and clergy, that they have a real knowledge of the Church of England and the character of its services, and a very sincere wish to be on friendly and brotherly terms with its members, clergy and laity alike. And I do not think there is one of them who would not consider it a great compliment and most kind attention if any English Churchman called upon him to pay his respects and show interest in his church and work.

Their keen interest in our Church all over the empire, even in a humble little village, is extraordinarily different from the almost complete ignorance and indifference which prevails amongst our own countrymen as to theirs, except amongst the members of one or two societies founded to bring the two Churches into more real unity of spirit.

However, this, like so many other things, is to be entirely changed. We are going to see and know more than we have ever done before of the way in which "God is working His purpose out" in His Church, as we are being brought into intelligent sympathy with a simply overwhelming part of Christendom, as represented by the Orthodox Church of Russia and the other Churches of the East.

Will there be many English Churchmen who will not be most deeply moved when they read that the first *Te Deum*, after all these centuries, has been sung in St. Sophia, in Constantinople? It will be a most inspiring thing too to hear that the whitewash, always peeling off, which covers up the mosaic picture of our *Lord*, has been cleared away, and He is shown looking down in blessing while the Holy Communion is once more celebrated in the great Church of Justinian.

We are all praying that *God* will bring good out of evil, and overcome evil with good, as this war draws on to its close, and many of us from time to time think of the "good" it will be for humanity if a more united Christian Church can be one of its first results. "Who will not pray?" said Mr. W. J. Birkbeck, the one English layman who knows Russia, its people, and its Church as few Englishmen or even Russians know them, when addressing a great gathering in London last year, "that this terrible conflict in which we are engaged will bring the Eastern and English Churches closer to one another? We are mindful of the considerable advances which have already been made in that direction, and of the ever-increasing friendship which has arisen between the English and Russian Churches of late years, and more especially during the twenty years' reign of the Emperor Nicholas II. It is known that even in the earliest years of his reign His Majesty more than once expressed his wish that the two Churches should get to know one another more closely, and that this was the best way to draw the two nations together. It is known too that Queen Victoria, when she was told of this, said, 'Yes, it is not only the best way, it is the only sure way.' The visits of Anglican bishops at various times have all tended to promote good feeling and mutual understanding, as did also the visit to England of the late Archbishop Antonius of Finland, afterwards Metropolitan of St. Petersburg, on the occasion of Queen Victoria's Diamond Jubilee. The question of the reunion of our two Churches is one that cannot be forced or rushed; it will never be brought about by compromises, or by diplomatic shams. It will only come about when the two Churches, after coming fully to know one another, find that both of them hold the whole of that Faith which each of them, and not one only, and all its members, and not some only, hold to be essential."

I hope it will not be uninteresting now if, as they are not many in number, I describe briefly the places where English Church work is carried on in Russia, and give some characteristic service at each.

At Petrograd the British Church, with the parsonage, library, and a number of other suites of rooms, is a great block of buildings, formerly a palace, owned and maintained by the British Factory, and with a staff of three clergy. The church is the former ballroom of the palace, and is a classical basilica, with rows of Greek pillars and capitals, and a very impressive place of worship. If I single out one of the beautiful services I have known I shall choose the Evensong on the Feast of the Epiphany last year, when I preached on the last day of my stay, and had what one might call a Sunday congregation. It was grand to see that large congregation on a weekday, so far away from home.

The Bishop and Russian Chauffeur in the midst of the Steppes on the way to Atbazar.

Three other places are served from Petrograd—Helsingfors, Narva, and Schlusselberg. Helsingfors has a small community of girls engaged in teaching and nursing, and the one Englishman who lives there with his wife, a Mr. Reid, is a Professor of English in the Finn University. One has to go there and return during the night, and during my day there I had a Confirmation in the Art School, most carefully and reverently prepared, and in the evening Mr. and Mrs. Reid had all the girls for a reception, at which I was able to chat with them individually and speak to them about the important and responsible trust they had in being allowed to lay the foundations of character in young lives. At midnight they were all on the station to say good-bye, bright English girls with sparkling eyes and happy faces. Who could not go away deeply thankful that they were not allowed to feel in that remote place that they were forgotten by their Church?

Narva is a great manufacturing community with a large staff of Englishmen, also a long journey away, and it so happens that they are nearly all Nonconformists there, but they value our services, and enjoyed mine with them, followed as it was by a special evening of music and recitations, about sixty being present.

Schlusselberg is a large factory for printing cotton goods for Asia, half a day's journey up the Neva, where we always have an evening service followed by Holy Communion next morning. It is the only place I have yet known where all the community, about forty, have been present at the evening service, and next morning been *all* present again as communicants, but with one added to their number, a man who had been away the night before.

Moscow has a church and parsonage and large courtyard, as will be seen in the illustration; almost startlingly like, it seems in that ancient capital, to a bit of a London suburb. But as I saw it on Christmas Eve last year it was Russian enough, the great courtyard was full of *troikas* and sledges, and the clear air musical with tinkling bells as the people came driving in from far and near, clad in warm furs, for the service. That Christmas Eve, with its carols and the old hymns, helped one to realize what it means to have an English church and clergyman in a community like that of Moscow. The chaplain conducts all the services, does all the work of the community, and visits over a large neighbourhood outside, single-handed.

Warsaw is the next capital to take, much before us of late, and perhaps with a great place yet to fill in future history. It is the centre of Christian work amongst the Russian Jews, as I shall have to explain more at length in my next chapter; but there is also a British community to whom the chaplain ministers, and which perhaps numbers, all told, about a hundred, with one or two outlying places reckoned in. The service I remember most at Warsaw, and shall always associate with it, was the dedication or consecration—the two abroad mean the same thing—of their church. We had it on a Sunday morning, with a very large congregation, and very impressive it was to take, so far away, as our little copies of the service told us, "The Order of Consecration as used in the Diocese of London." There were some Old Catholics present, and they were deeply impressed with the scriptural character of a service which carried us back to the days of David and Solomon. I dare say it was true of all there, as one of them said, that they had never seen the consecration of a church of their own before, and had had to come to Russia for it when they did.

We have only two other places in our jurisdiction—as the shores of the Black Sea fall to the Diocese of Gibraltar—Libau and Riga.

Libau is a Baltic port in Courland, a German-speaking place, where there is an extremely small British community, but where there are a fair number of British ships in the course of the year. The establishment consists of two flats side by side, one of which supplies the chaplain and his wife with a comfortable home; and the other, which communicates with it, provides an institute, with papers and a billiard-table, etc., for the sailors, and a beautiful little chapel opening out of it. When last there we had a reception, or social, in the institute, followed by a service; after which we came back into the institute, and I had a talk with the seamen and apprentices and one or two young fellows in the business houses. I need not ask the reader if he thinks that little church ought to be there or not.

Riga is a great port, also on the Baltic, and its beautiful church, with a great spire, is close to the banks of the river. It has a splendid position and is tremendously appreciated and well supported by a fairly large and prosperous community. The service to mention here was my Confirmation on the Russian Whitsun Day last year but one. Every one comes to a Confirmation abroad, and it was to us at Riga a real anniversary of the great gift of the HOLY SPIRIT. It was in the afternoon, and we had had the Holy Communion at eight and Morning Service at eleven as at home—but the Confirmation was at three, and was *the* service of the day.

It makes a great difference when a large congregation can really be brought to pray during the short space of silence usually kept for the purpose. They most certainly prayed that afternoon at Riga, and many told me in touching language what an experience it had been to them. These are *great* opportunities abroad. A man in middle life told me once, also abroad, what the confirmation of his daughter had been to him that day after he had been led specially to pray in the service; and he added, "I've never been at a Confirmation before this since my own at Charterhouse, and I can only wish that it had meant more to me at the time."

There is one other place to mention, the port which is historic for us in more senses than one just now—Archangel. It is not actually upon the White Sea, but a little distance up the Dvina, and is frequented by a good number of British ships in the summer when the sea there is free from ice. There is a church and a rectory, but no community at all, and so the Russia Company send a chaplain there for the summer months to visit the men aboard ship and hold services for them ashore.

The Anglican Church in Russia, therefore, for I have described every place in which it is at work, is not a very large community, but I can claim that it is zealous, earnest, efficient, and thoroughly representative, and I feel sure that it will be admitted that it is doing a real and good work for Russia as well as for ourselves. I have often brought home to myself the real significance of an interest or influence by asking myself what I should do without it. And if one only just thinks, "What would our countrymen do in Russia? how would they hope to knit up real and lasting ties, if their Church were not there?" there would be, to my mind, no answer which could be adequately expressed in words.

I hope to be able, when the war is over, to appoint a chaplain whose work it shall be to travel over those great spaces in European and Siberian Russia and visit very small communities where it is impossible for a permanent chaplain to find enough to do.

These will rapidly increase now as the country and its people become better known to us. The first Church of England Service ever taken in Siberia is a very good instance to give of such opportunities. It was in 1912, at Ekaterinburg, just beyond the Urals, and in the government of Perm, a large and growing town of 80,000 people, where our British community is represented almost entirely by one family named Yates, paper manufacturers, whose first mill was built there fifty years ago. It now consists of Mr. and Mrs. Yates, their brothers, children, and grandchildren.

Ekaterinburg is a distributing centre for the Bible Society, and their agent—earnest, energetic, and capable—is one of the best-known and respected Englishmen in Siberia. He it was who had prepared for my coming, arranged for me to stay with Mr. and Mrs. Yates, and invited every one within reach—"I've sounded the big drum," he said—and with governesses, English wives of Russians, a young fellow and his wife teaching roller-skating, and one or two others—some having travelled long distances to get there—we must have numbered about thirty in all. They prepared a little temporary altar in the large drawing-room, with an *ikon*, flowers, etc., and we had Holy Communion, a morning and evening service, our dinner and supper together, and a priceless experience of the unity which thankfulness and fellowship always bring with them when realized in common prayer and worship.

From Ekaterinburg I went a day's journey to another town, in a part of the country to which very few English travellers ever go, and there the small community consisted of one family only, though they were three generations. We were only a dozen altogether, and some might think it was hardly worth taking up a bishop's time for three days to go and see one family. But the head of that family had been there between forty and fifty years, and never had our Church's service during that time, nor received Communion. The grandchildren had never seen or heard the service before, and they were the children of a Russian father, attending a Russian school. I made my address simple so that they could understand it, knowing that the others could if the children did, and I had one or two opportunities of conversation with them, which they greatly welcomed. Late at night I left, all the party accompanying me to the station to see me off; and after we had said, "Good-bye," and they had left, the mother of those children came back quietly and said:—

"Bishop, I felt I must come back just to tell you this. In the winter, after having tried so long to keep my boy and girl English in their ideas, I felt hopeless and gave up the struggle; but I want you to know that in the service to-day I've had the strength and courage given me to begin again."

The British Community at Atbazar, Siberia, after Morning Service during the Bishop's Visit.

Is it not worth while to have a travelling chaplain go about and find such experiences as that waiting for him in many places? Can any one possibly think that those who have to live on the Continent of Europe, because of some fanciful ideas of intrusion upon the jurisdiction of another Church, should be deprived of the services of their own, and find, as they inevitably do find, that they are ever accepting for themselves a lowered standard and a dimmer ideal?

I remember a girl whom I had confirmed in Switzerland coming at a later visit to tell me that, after six months of happy life as a communicant, she had begun to "fall away," and now seemed to have "lost all interest." What was she to do? On being questioned, it appeared that at the end of those six months she had gone to stay with a family in the country, where there was no English church within any possible distance, and she said:—

"I missed the services at first, but I *found gradually that I could do without them*; and so I grew not to mind." I advised her, wherever she was in future, when not able to attend a service, carefully to use the Communion Office at eight o'clock, and think of all those who were in church, and realize her unity with them, and reverently and slowly think over all the special parts of the service, and she would find herself eager enough to go to church at the usual time when opportunity again presented itself, as she would have wished every time she was reading the service that she was having the complete experience. She would not "find that she could do without it." Spiritual things are spiritually discerned. And if we drop away from those means of grace which help us to be spiritually minded, there will certainly in time be little, if any, spiritual experiences to show.

This chapter is not, like the others, concerned with Russian people and affairs; but I have ventured to write it because without it English Churchmen would not be able to understand fully the influence we are exercising upon Russian life and thought even now, and which, in far fuller measure, we are expecting to exercise in the time to come.

The Duma (I was assured in 1911 when calling at the Ministry of the Interior in Petrograd) have been preparing a Bill for some time to give the Anglican Church in Russia a legal status and recognition such as it has never yet had! We shall be glad and thankful enough to have it, but I am far more happy and grateful in the thought of the real *spiritual* influence our Church possesses and exercises, even without that legal status, both in the permanent chaplaincies and in those distant places visited from time to time.

Just as in its legislation, it is not so much the law as it stands which determines the state of things social in Russia, as the trend and aim and purpose of every new enactment, and the present actual life of the people. All that is in one direction in Russia. Government becomes ever more and more constitutional. It is the same with respect to religious life and prospects. There has been no change whatever in the actual formal and legal relations of the Russian and Anglican Churches; but surely and evidently, in sympathy, mutual knowledge, regard, and respect, every year, they are drawing more closely and affectionately together.

I cannot close this chapter without expressing my deep and grateful appreciation of the help and support given to our work by the Russia Society. It is no longer a trading company but still possesses large funds and, it seems to me, they must all be spent in support of our Anglican Church in Russia. It is impossible even to think of what that work would be without the help given to us by the Russia Society, and the British Factory in Petrograd.

FOOTNOTES:

[13] *Contemporary Review*, November, 1914.

CHAPTER XI
THE JEWS

The Jewish question was the first of many I was called upon to consider after crossing the Russian frontier, for my first service within the empire was the Confirmation of a Jew. He was of the educated class, and particularly attractive; and as he bowed low over my hand and kissed it with a singular grace of manner the western part of Europe seemed already far away. It was at Warsaw, where, as at Cracow—the ancient capital of Poland—the Jews form a larger and more influential part of the population than in any other European city. It will surprise many, no doubt, to hear that, though the Anglican Church has no *legal* status as yet, our chaplain at Warsaw has the sole and exclusive right of baptizing those Jews who are Russian subjects, and wish to be received into the Christian Church. *Any* Jew who wishes to become a Christian, if in the Russian Empire, must go to Warsaw and receive Baptism from the Anglican chaplain, maintained there for many years by the London Society for Promoting Christianity among the Jews.

The Archbishop of Warsaw.

This young Russian, with his wife, had travelled a great distance for his Baptism and Confirmation, and, if I remember rightly, was leaving Russia in the course of time. He was able, therefore, to receive Confirmation in our own Church, although Russian subjects, if Jewish, on receiving Baptism from us—it is a strange anomaly that we hope will soon cease—are expected to choose whether they will next be received into the communion of the Lutheran, Roman Catholic, or Orthodox Churches. None of these, of course, attract them after receiving instruction and Baptism in our own Church, and, on that account, no doubt, many of them have reverted again to their old religion.

The passport system in Russia is an admirable and comprehensive one, and as soon as a Hebrew Christian abandons his Faith and returns to Judaism, he is required by law to report it at once to the local authority, in order that his passport may be altered; and on his doing so a notice is at once dispatched to our chaplain at Warsaw that a pen is to be drawn through his name in the baptismal register. It was painfully affecting to turn over the pages of that register, and see those ominous-looking lines drawn from top to bottom of various entries. One could not see anything like it anywhere else, I suppose. It carried the mind back to the early days of the Faith, and to that sad class known as the *lapsi* ("lapsed"); to the lament over Demas, who had forsaken S. Paul and gone back to the world; and to such promises as "I will not blot out his name from the book of life."

There is much in the work at Warsaw to take one back thus in spirit to the days of the Apostles. One felt it a little at the Confirmation itself, when saying the sentence which accompanies the laying on of hands, first in German for the young Jew, and then in English for the girl who followed him; but most of all on the Sunday evening, when the services of the day in the little chapel were all over, and everything was quiet.

That is the time always given to "inquirers"; and they came one after another, that first Sunday of mine at Warsaw, stealing in, just as Nicodemus came by night and for the same reason, sometimes singly, sometimes husband and wife together, and sometimes a whole family—the children going off to join the chaplain's children, while the parents came to us. When the room in time was quite full we began by singing a few hymns in German, after which the chaplain prayed for guidance and the sense of God's presence; and then a most interesting time followed. He took the holy Gospel for the day, every one reading a verse in turn—in German—during which questions were encouraged if the literal meaning of the verse was not clear.

It was a particularly arresting Gospel for those present to consider, as it included our LORD'S words, "If I by the finger of GOD cast out devils, no doubt the kingdom of GOD is come upon you." There is no more striking symbol for a Jew than that of the "finger of GOD," nor anything more absorbingly interesting than "GOD'S kingdom"; and I have always thankfully felt that I was fortunate that night. The Chaplain of Warsaw is not one who loses or wastes opportunities, and he did his very best with that one. It was an extraordinarily interesting scene as I watched the faces of that little gathering of men and women gazing with the keenest and most penetrating of expressions upon their teacher; and now and then, as he mentioned psalm or prophecy, taking up their Bibles to find the passage named. Then, satisfied as to its apposite character, they would look up again as eagerly as before. I seemed to be back again in spirit sharing in one of those Apostolic scenes of the New Testament, when one or another "preached CHRIST unto them," and they, as at Berea, received the teaching "with readiness of mind, and searched the Scriptures whether those things were so."

Just such little gatherings as that at Warsaw, and in just such places, to which people came stealthily yet expectantly, were addressed by Barnabas and Paul, by Silas and John Mark. One feels now when listening to a chapter from the Acts of the Apostles, or reading it, as if one had been there and seen and heard. It is only a year since I was once more at Warsaw, and again it was Sunday evening, with the Holy Communion, Confirmation, and other services of the day all over, and just as before the Jewish inquirers came quietly in, in ones and twos and threes, only this time the gathering was larger and the attention keener even than it had been three years before. The same order was followed, the singing of hymns in German, prayer—those present were encouraged to pray in very simple words—the reading of a passage from the New Testament, and then its exposition; but though it was the same faithful teaching of the Faith, or preaching CHRIST, there was a difference both in what was said and in the questions asked. It was no longer the Messiah, or the CHRIST fulfilling Messianic psalm or evangelical prophecy, but the living CHRIST of to-day.

It was a sight not soon, if ever, to be forgotten, those keen Jewish faces, such as our LORD Himself looked into daily during His ministry, eager, expectant, hopeful, while questioning again, as in the Synagogue of Capernaum, how it could be possible for Him to be not only Way and Truth, but *Life*; how He could in any comprehensible sense be said to *live* in His people, and how any one could with any conviction say or sing "And now I live in Him." It made one feel that even there, in far-away and comparatively unknown Russia, that same Spirit is moving upon the waters to whom the *Quarterly Review* gave its testimony in the October number of 1912, when it stated at the close of a remarkable review of modern German and other critical literature that the net result of modern negative criticism had only been "to make the living CHRIST a greater Reality to-day than He has been since the days of the Apostles." So it was at Warsaw that night. They wanted to understand the CHRIST whom S. Paul not only taught but had *experienced* ever since his conversion, and which enabled and impelled him to say, "I live, yet not I, but CHRIST liveth in me."

The Jews have had hard experiences in Russia, and the story of their wrongs would take long to tell; but let us hope that now there is no reason for wishing to tell it. We are hoping that in more ways than one Russia is going to "forget those things which are behind, and reach forward to those things which are before," and which are worthy of the aims of a great nation. Few nobler things have been said during the war than General Botha's counsel to his fellow-countrymen when the Beyers and De Wet revolution had come to a fitting end. He reminded them that what had happened was within their own household, and their own affair, and that the only right course was to let by-gones be by-gones, and "cultivate a spirit of tolerance and forbearance and merciful oblivion" with respect to the errors of the past.

A year ago, if writing upon Russian life of to-day, one could not but have touched upon the hardships of the Jews who have to live "within the pale" in Russia, and have been alternately tolerated and persecuted, even massacred within recent years; and one would have had to own that there was something to be said upon the Russian side as well, even if not agreeing with it. But this is now no longer necessary. In Russia as in South Africa we must say, "Let by-gones be by-gones, and let the spirit of tolerance and forbearance and merciful oblivion" blot out the errors of the past for Russian and for Jew. It should be remembered also that the devout Jew is as mystical in his religion as the Russian, who must surely now and then, as he looks toward the seven-branched candlestick within his own sacrarium, or listens to the psalms, be reminded that his devotion has a Jewish source.

A Jewish Confirmation with none but Jews in the congregation is a great experience. Twice I have had it at Wandsbeck, just outside Hamburg, where, under Pastor Dolman of our London Society, the work is entirely for and amongst Jews. At my first visit there were about fourteen candidates, fine young men from many countries, one or two being German and Austrian, and several in uniform. As we entered, the large congregation, without rising, began to sing a German hymn, slowly and softly, and at once the whole atmosphere of the place became deeply devotional. Everything was in German, and though I confirm in German I cannot venture to preach or address in the language; and so in the address Pastor Dolman stood beside me to interpret, and so masterly and rapid was this interpretation that the candidates seemed to be listening to me, rather than to him, from first to last. There was no mistaking the spirit of that congregation, nor the character of the service. Every one was in it, every one deeply interested and attentive, and eager to be spiritually helped. The consciousness of it seemed to embrace every one present in the most convincing way, and again seemed to carry us back to Apostolic days, making one wonder whether amongst those rugged and strong-featured men and women there might not be another Aquila and Priscilla, ready for work if God should bring it to them; whether amongst those youths there might not be another Timotheus ready to gladden the heart of any one who should see what was in him and take him in hand for GOD. "Why shouldn't there be amongst this eager-looking crowd," I found myself thinking, "another Apollos, or even a S. Paul?"

A Polish Jew.

I shall always be glad also to have visited Cracow, and taken a service there in what we shall probably soon be speaking of as "the old days before the war." Nowhere, I suppose, in Europe does the Jew walk the streets of a city with the same confidence and assurance as he does in this ancient capital of Poland and burial-place of its kings. The Jews form a very large part of its population, fill the foremost places of commercial importance, and show most unmistakably in every look and gesture how strong, whenever it can find expression, is the Jewish pride of race.

There is a very small Christian community both here and at Lemberg—or Luow as we must call it now—but there are two licensed laymen to deal with Jewish inquirers, and we had a celebration of Holy Communion, and conference together two years ago. I saw then another side of the Russian or Polish Jew, for whether he is in Poland proper or that part of the old kingdom which is called Galicia, or in the western part of Russia—he is not legally allowed anywhere else in the empire—the Jew, of course, is always essentially the same.

It is most important to keep this from slipping out of sight when thinking of them. I was reading a short time ago a most depressing account of life in some Jewish villages in a certain part of Russia, of the dirt and degradation of the people there, their cunning and greed, their hang-dog expression of countenance, and disgusting clothing. Every one is familiar with the stories told of the usurer and the extortioner who suck the blood of their inexperienced and unsuspecting victims, and it is not for me to question their accuracy. We may all admit that Shylock is a type. But still environment plays its part, and it would be difficult to picture any other result from the treatment which has been meted out to Jews in Russia than the degradation which has followed.

A very different picture, however, is given for us by Mr. Rothay Reynolds, in the report of a *Russian* official, sent out by his government to visit the settlements of Russian Jews in the Argentine Republic. He made a formal report, but it was no dry and formal statement, but a real picture, painted in glowing colours, of the "change wrought in them by the free and open life of the new land," and he described with enthusiasm the rich farms possessed and admirably cultivated by the former children of the *ghetto*. He drew a contrast between the peaky, timorous Jewish boys of the Russian pale and the lusty Jewish youngsters astride half-tamed horses on the ranche. And the settlers spoke of Russia as our colonists speak of the old country, as "home." No Jew *in Russia* dreams of calling himself a Russian, but when he goes and settles in another land far away, and prospers there, then he can speak of Russia as "home."

There are 6,000,000 Jews in the empire, and 250,000 of them rallied to the colours, we are told, at the general mobilization. It may be claimed, therefore, that they have "done their bit." Will this count for nothing after the war? We are assured by one authority after another that the war only precipitated the proclamation of autonomy for Poland, and gave it wider application and comprehension. We are told, and I for one believe it, that the government have been preparing for some time to give constitutional rule to Finland as well as to Poland, and that the old idea of "Russifaction" is entirely abandoned and set aside. All this is in keeping with what has followed, in some cases swiftly, in others slowly, but in all important matters which concern the well-being of the state, *in some measure or other*, since 1905. This being so we should expect that the Jews will also be admitted before long to equal civil and political rights with other Russian subjects of the Emperor, and I feel sure the hopes will not be disappointed. The Jewish revolutionaries in the past have been the most dangerous of all, and I believe there has never been any conspiracy of real moment in which they have not taken a share; but there again, as we think of their degradation in country villages, we cannot but ask, "How could anything else be expected of them? Treated as they have been, their boldest spirits would be sure to plot." The Jews with us are loyal and patriotic citizens and though proud—as they have a right to be—of their race, they are proud also of their nationality. So it will be in Russia when she gives them freedom. None will be more patriotic than they, amongst all the mixed races which make up the empire. They have given a foretaste of this already. A writer in the *Contemporary Review* last December

(Gabriel Costa), in telling us something of what "Freeing Six Millions" would mean, points out that while no Russian Jewish soldier could hold commissioned rank, nor aspire even to be the conductor of a military band—though none could be more fitted—nor be accepted as an army surgeon, yet when the call to arms came great numbers of Jewish doctors were summoned to the front, and obeyed the call. He also tells us how Jews of all social grades contributed freely to the Red Cross funds, whilst—most wonderful of all—the Jews of Kishineff, where one of the most terrible of all Russia's *"pogroms"* or massacres (the word means literally destruction) took place, offered up prayers in its synagogues for the success of the Russian army.

It is a very significant and instructive fact of life that where great issues have to be faced together, whether it is by few or many, those barriers which have been considered fundamental, of race, religion, and politics, have a strange way of disappearing and sinking out of sight. Sometimes it is disconcerting, but often it is most encouraging and even inspiring. And so when Jews are confronted by the tremendous issues of this war they find that they can pray for those towards whom but lately they have been burning with a deep sense of indignant wrong. Russians and Poles have been at enmity together for generations now, but in face of the common peril and the common foe all this is forgotten, and the Russian officers sent to head-quarters soon after the invasion of Poland their grateful recognition of the heroism of the Polish peasant children who made a regular practice of carrying water to the Russian trenches, often under fire and at imminent peril of their lives, while steadfastly refusing all payment. So with Jew and Christian. The death of the Chief Rabbi of Lyons on the battle-field has been told in papers all over the world since it first appeared, last October, in the *Jewish World*. "The Chief Rabbi was bringing spiritual consolation to the wounded Jewish soldiers on the battle-field, when he was called to the side of a dying Roman Catholic trooper. The dying man, evidently mistaking the rabbi for a priest of his own faith, begged him to hold the crucifix before his eyes and to give him his blessing. While holding a crucifix and whispering words of comfort to the mortally wounded soldier the rabbi was shot dead!" No less appealing and encouraging for those who long to see nationalities and great races appreciating and admiring each other's national temperaments and racial characteristics are some of the incidents which Gabriel Costa gives us in his *Freeing Six Millions*.

> "First to attract notice," he says, "is the exploit of a Jewish medical student from Wilna, named Osnas, invalided home on account of wounds received in saving the colours of his regiment during the fighting in East Prussia. 'Do everything that is possible to save the life of Osnas,' telegraphed his

commander to the hospital authorities. The medical student has been honoured by the bestowal of the military Cross of S. George.

"When events come to be sifted, we shall probably hear of similar instances of Russo-Jewish patriotism. As for our own brave soldiers, there can be nothing more convincing, nothing more gratifying than the emphatic reply of a wounded corporal of the Black Watch to a 'voice' in a crowd of sympathetic Londoners. 'And the Jews,' queried the 'voice,' 'What are they doing?' The Highlander replied, without a moment's hesitation, 'Doing? Well, their duty. We had three with us, and bonnier lads and braver I don't wish to see. They fought just splendid.'

"No less arresting was the avowal of a private of the Berkshire Regiment. 'We had ten in our company,' he said, 'all good fighters, and six won't be seen again. So don't say a word against the Jews.'"

Why has Russia's attitude hitherto, then, been, and for so long, one of rigid exclusion? The Pale, to which they are limited, includes only the ten provinces of Russian Poland, and fifteen provinces in Western Russia, and the arrangements were made first by the government of Catherine the Great in 1791, and definitely settled in 1835. Even there, though by law they are entitled to live and follow their particular tastes and callings freely, yet we are told that "harassing laws restrict their initiative and make even their right of residence within the Pale itself become something of a chimera." Why is this policy of vexatious exclusion so persistently followed? We are told that it is because the Jewish element is a sordid and deteriorating influence, bad for the local and national life alike, and a hindrance to the nation's progress. This, however, was clearly not the view of M. de Plehve when, as Minister of the Interior, he received a deputation of representative Jews petitioning for an extension of civil rights. He is reported to have said to them, "It is not true that the Tsar and myself regard the Jews as an inferior race. On the contrary, we regard them as exceptionally smart and clever. But if we admitted Jews to our universities, without restriction, they would overshadow our own Russian students and dominate our own intellectual life. I do not think it would be fair to allow the minority thus to obtain an advantage over the majority in this way." He did not seem to see that, as those in question were *Russian subjects*, the very ability to which he gave his testimony was being prevented from enriching the national life. This is a fallacy as old as history itself, and pursued by that shortsighted Pharaoh on the Nile of whom it is significantly said, by way of explanation of his folly, that "He knew not Joseph!" As we read the records of Scripture—and the historical books are for the most part extraordinarily dispassionate and free from undue Hebrew bias—we see that neither Egypt, Assyria, Chaldea, nor Persia had any cause to regret giving Jews a place in their national life, and that their fatal mistakes, even with the Jews themselves, lay in *not* following Jewish counsels.

The Jews have what can only be called a genius for patriotism, and in a way not to be explained they breathe in this spirit very deeply towards any nation which bids them welcome, and offers them a home. During my first service in Siberia, described in another chapter, at Ekaterinburg, three years ago, a young soldier in Russian uniform walked slowly into the room, and took his place with a most wondering expression on his face. He was, I found, a young Jew, and had received baptism some time before in England. The manœuvres had brought him to that part of Siberia, and to his great amazement he had heard just before, that in that unlikely place, there was to be on the following Sunday a service of the Church into which he had been baptized. In my conversation with him afterwards, however, it seemed to me that I was speaking not to a Jew but to a Russian. Somewhere, no doubt, he is fighting now, and as patriotically, I feel sure, as his comrades in the ranks. Is it good policy to waste such good material as this, to restrict the national assets in this way, and keep back its powers of expansion and development? To ask such questions in these days is to answer them.

> "I have been discussing," says Mr. Costa in his most instructive article, "with Jewish folk in London, Russian men and women of culture and refinement, the prospect of this dream becoming a reality. They incline to the belief that if Russia is really in earnest over the matter, and is not propounding it as a strategical move; if, in our time, she will hurl to the dust the grim, hope-excluding walls of the congested Pale, she cannot but open up an era of unexampled greatness and prosperity. With that wonderful intellectual force, now held in check, applied to the advancement of Russian culture and progress, the Empire of the Tsar might awaken and expand beyond the most ambitious dreams of its dead-and-gone autocrats."

Just as we are led to believe that a people gets the government it deserves, so we may well be brought to think that possibly, with respect to this virile and persistent race, the nation gets the Jews it deserves. As a policy which is meant to degrade must have a degraded class as its result, so to give every part of the nation's life and equipment full equality of opportunity is to get the best the nation as a whole has to give in return. We are further told by Mr. Costa that while the Russian conscript fights because he must, the English Jew fights because he loves to serve the country which has been all in all to him and his. And thus "Peer's son and first-born of the *ghetto* grocer rub shoulders in the task of upholding the nation's honour. In the Regulars, Cavalry, Guards, and Territorials, here you shall find the cream of Anglo-Jewry, the sons of merchant princes, men who hold the purse-strings of nations."

I suppose there is no country in the world where so long and so freely, as with us, the Jews have been able to give their full contribution to the national life, and who amongst us with any breadth of view and largeness of heart does not see what this has meant to us in the past, and is meaning for us just now?

If any race can truthfully say that they have never had a chance that race is the Jews. They have not even had a proper chance of accepting Christianity. The Christian Church marvellously soon became their enemy. The nations of the world, without exception, since the first destruction of Jerusalem have taken up the same position of antagonism. All this could only have one end.

In the new time to come, let all this be forgotten, and the nations use all their national life to the full, and confidently await the result. Nothing to my mind can withstand the influence of our Christian religion when it is presented as the religion of *Christ* Himself; and the modern Jew, I for one believe, will find it as hard to go on kicking against the pricks as his great co-religionist did when he encountered the real thing in S. Stephen, and was already prepared to receive it as his own experience. Nothing can stifle loyal and dutiful service in the hearts of her children when a nation is a true mother to them all. This, in Church and State, we can honestly claim is our own aim towards the Jews; let us express the Emperor's confident hope once more, and say, "Some day it will be like that in Russia."

CHAPTER XII
OUR COUNTRYMEN IN THE EMPIRE

"There are no two powers in the world—and there have been no other two in history—*more* distinct in character, *less* conflicting in interests, and more naturally *adapted* for mutual agreement and support than are Britain and Russia."

It is in the full endorsement of these carefully-weighed statements, from a most experienced authority, that I wish to write this last chapter. Looking back upon the past to the days of Ivan the Terrible and Queen Elizabeth, and reviewing the situation in the Russian Empire to-day, and, above all, looking forward to our immediate future, it seems to me that our countrymen in Russia have had a real mission to fulfil, and have done it worthily and well.

They have, from the first, prepared the ground for what has come up for a great decision to-day, our splendid opportunity of having Russia for a friend. And they have not done it by working and planning, still less by scheming for it, but, just as we should wish our countrymen to extend our influence the world over, by being honestly and consistently true to their own nationality, and worthily representing British traditions and ideals.

There is one testimony, if I may venture without undue complacency to give it, to the estimation in which our nationality is held, which does not suggest that we are really considered, even by those who have of late so often glibly said it, to be degenerate and decadent and not fit to hold the possessions we have, or shape the destinies of the many peoples who own our rule. I have never met any one yet, of another nationality, who did not think it a compliment to be mistaken for an Englishman. It is not often that one can make such a mistake, but I have met Dutchmen and Germans, and Russians also, who just for a moment or two, from dress, expression, or speech have made one feel that they were fellow countrymen. Young Russians especially, though different in physique, for often they are built on huge lines and are enormously strong, after receiving an English education from a very early age, wearing English dress, being pleased to meet us, may easily be considered to be English; and I doubt if there are amongst them any who would not feel it a compliment to be so considered, while they would resent the same mistake being made with regard to any other nationality.

Englishmen, therefore, it will be admitted, have kept up the standard in Russia, and not let down the good name of their own country. When I was visiting the Troitsk Gold Mine, in 1912—a little short of three days' and three nights' journey, on the other side of Moscow—to spend Sunday and give them their first English services, the surveyor, when showing me over the mine and its workings on the Monday, told me that those large illustrated almanacks which we have, with a picture in the middle and information about Church and parish round the sides, and which are so often seen on the walls of the houses of our own working-classes, are also very popular amongst their own work-people.

"They are got up in the Russian style, of course," he said, "with a Russian illustration, and so on; but you will be interested to hear that a great part of the paragraphs round it is given up to describing English ways and ideas, societies and arrangements, and always with appreciation and approval."

It must ever be remembered that people who cannot leave their own country must judge largely of other countries by what they see of those who come from them. If English ideas, manners, and customs are held in favour and esteem in Russia and Siberia it can only be, therefore, because English men and women have worthily represented them there in business and commerce, by upright and moral conduct.

It does not usually fall to the lot of a bishop in these days, many-sided as are his sympathies, and various as are the claims made upon his time and attention, to see much of actual business and commercial life, nor have I seen much of the working of factories and workshops in the other countries in our jurisdiction; but in Russia and Siberia one of the most important parts of a visitation has been the going amongst the members of a staff while they were actually at work so as to get to really know them and their daily lives.

Outside Moscow, for instance, are nearly twenty mills and manufactories; in and outside Petrograd are some of the largest and best-managed cotton and thread-mills in the world; at Schlusselberg, on the Neva, there is a large and splendidly equipped print-works for Asiatic trade; at Narva, a day's journey from Petrograd, is a huge factory employing some 70,000 people; and in Siberia are the great mining enterprises, some of them employing from 18,000 to 20,000 people of both sexes. And in all these places the staff is composed of our own countrymen, and numbers, sometimes as many as sixty.

I have always, in these places, stayed with the manager, and have had opportunities of meeting the staff socially and for services, going into every department in the mill, factory, or mine, and, as these visits were not short, making friends and learning their experiences, seeing their outlook and often acquiring the history of the enterprise, with all its ups and downs, and successes and failures, from the very first. Then I am a guest always at the Embassy in Petrograd, and am asked to meet all who can be brought together by kind and courteous host and hostess. It is the same with the Consul and his wife in other cities. And above all is it so when I am the guest of the chaplain, who takes care that I meet every one in the community who cares about it. I get thus into close touch with all sorts and conditions of men, and am compelled to come to the conclusion that very few can have anything like the opportunity of really knowing, in a general way, his own countrymen in Russia as the bishop who goes amongst them. It seems to me, therefore, to be a very real duty to give my tribute to what they have done to make England well spoken of and well thought of throughout the empire.

Englishmen have succeeded amongst the Russians for precisely the same reason that they have succeeded in building up vast colonies and a huge empire. They have developed, and not exploited. There is a way of becoming rich by exploiting resources at the expense of those employed. Instances will occur to the reader at once, and probably are not far to seek. I myself have seen this degrading process conducted on a fairly large scale in another hemisphere, while the most terrible and sinister instance of all is that of the Congo, out of which King Leopold and his agents amassed an immense fortune in a few years, while the natives engaged in collecting the rubber were reduced from twenty millions to a little over seven. No more deadly and wicked *exploitation* was ever known.

True *development*, on the other hand, is cultivating and bringing into use the resources of a country and improving the conditions of life for those who produce them at the same time. We have been accused again and again, even by writers of our own, of exploiting India, and of being indifferent to the true interests of its people. No one has ever known, for the Hindoo temperament is vastly different from our own, whether its people did not think so too. But the war has declared it. When India rose as one man and asked only to be allowed to give all for those who had ruled them, then we all knew that we had been understood all over that vast dependency of ours as being there not only to get but to give, not to exploit but to develop.

Is it not true of Egypt also, where the *fellaheen* along the Nile are of the same race in general habits and employments as their ancestors of thousands of years ago, though different ruling races have come and gone, that in all those ages they have never enjoyed true liberty, and never reaped the fruit of their labours and toil without oppression until they came under British rule? It need not weigh at all with us that this is not known or acknowledged, as it ought to be in Egypt. We are not given, fortunately, to worrying as to what other people think about us. Perhaps it might be better for us sometimes if we were. But we know that in time Egypt will learn, as India has learnt, that we are amongst them not to exploit them, but to develop their resources and to improve in every way that is possible their own character and condition. Thus has it been also in Russia; and I felt a very thankful man, proud of my country and nationality, when, a year ago, I could say to the Emperor of Russia, "My countrymen are in Siberia, sir, not to exploit but to help to develop Russia's resources and its people."

"I know it," he quietly said. And I gave him the following instance to show him how rapidly and on what a large scale this is being done.

Some distance to the left of the Orenburg line which runs down from Samara to Tashkend in Turkestan, and not far from Orenburg itself, only reached at present by motor-car and camel, is a place called Tanalyk, an English property. Not much more than a year ago there were there a British engineer, surveyor, and assistants, with a little handful of nomads, Kirghiz I should think, looking on and giving their labour. They were engaged in prospecting, and drilling for copper. Now, even in this short time, the preliminary work of a great mine has been begun, and there are from eighteen to twenty thousand Russians engaged in it. Accommodation has been provided, schools are going up, their church and priest are there, medical and surgical treatment is within the reach of all. There are stores where they can buy everything they need in the way of food, dress, appliances, all sorts of conveniences and comforts that they have never seen before, at prices which give no profit to the company. Those who used to taste meat perhaps once a fortnight can have it daily, for they have good wages. They are becoming more handy as workmen and improved in physique, and the next generation will be better still. Education and the amenities of life are increasing their self-respect. The determination of the staff not to overlook bad work, their wish to see them improve in character, to set them an example in their own family life, are all having their effect. "Is it possible," I asked, "to put too high a value on such good work as this which adds to Russia's enterprise, wealth, and resources, and makes all those thousands of men, women, and children better subjects of your Majesty and the empire?"

The managing director of the Russo-Asiatic Corporation, which began its development with Tanalyk, and has gone on to other and more important developments still, told me that when local option was granted, two years ago, he himself was given the sole right of deciding whether those thousands of Russians should have *vodka* or not, although it was at that time a government monopoly, and important as a source of revenue. He decided that *vodka* should not be sold, but that a very light and harmless beer might be provided for those who wished to have it. It was only to be sold by one man, however, and if an instance of drunkenness occurred he was to lose his right to sell. The amount paid for rent has been spent on a People's House for the recreation of all employed at the mine.

Camels at Work—Summer.

Another manager friend of mine told me that he had helped his people to become more sober by selling *vodka* at his own stores at a lower price than that of the government. It sounds a strange way of doing it, no doubt, but the sale was restricted to Wednesdays and Saturdays. When, therefore, on the other days there came would-be purchasers anxious to have *vodka*, with the plea that there was a wedding or a christening or some other domestic festivity at which it would be needed just to complete the enjoyment, they were always told that they could not have it except on the stated days. This was not hardship, for the government shop was open, though the higher price was demanded there. This they would not pay and so went without it, and yet the christening or wedding passed off no less happily—perhaps even more happily; and thus, gradually, amongst the Russian staff, and through them the work-people, there grew up the idea that the results of *vodka* were to be avoided.

Nothing could be more encouraging than the experience of the management of this particular mine in trying, by example and discipline, to lift their foremen and subordinates of the staff out of what used to be thought a perfectly natural and pardonable weakness, but now throughout the empire is being acknowledged as a national sin.

It will surely and easily be seen by any thinking reader that this initiative on the one hand, and responsiveness on the other, promise well for our future relations with each other, and explains, perhaps, how the Russian *Entente* has passed quite naturally into an Alliance, which some of us hope and believe will be permanent and stable for many generations.

Our *Entente* with France has been indeed an *Entente Cordiale*, and it is now more cordial and friendly than ever; but it is not easy to conceive of anything in the future beyond an *Entente* and Alliance. We can be real and staunch and faithful friends as becomes those who are near neighbours, but little else opens out before us. Is it possible to think of anything between ourselves and Germany, even when the war is over and many years have passed, except the gradual removal of sadly embittered feelings and outraged convictions and beliefs? Our ideas of what can rightly be called world-power and world-forces are so diametrically opposed that it passes the imagination of man to conceive what great world-purpose we and they could undertake together, for some time.

But directly we think of ourselves and Russia as side by side, and with confidence in each other, there is no limit to what we and they may hope to accomplish together for our own peoples, for humanity, and for GOD. Not only have we constitutional and religious ideals in common, but our own countrymen are already at work all over the richest and most promising part of their vast empire, and upon the only right lines any one can adopt if the object in view is to increase the resources, character, and ability of a people at the same time.

The Englishman of the ordinary and normal type cannot be content to look upon the man he employs as merely a wage-earner. He wants, as he would put it, "to give him a leg-up" besides, and our countrymen in Siberia have sought just to give that "leg-up" to their employs, to better their conditions of life and educate their children; by precept and example to give them wholesome recreations; to help them to see that there is nothing laughable but everything that is disgusting in such a vice as drunkenness; and to help them in every way they can to manly self-respect.

This is tremendously far-reaching in its results. The Christian paradox is fulfilled here also. "To lose is to save, to save is to lose." To try and get all one can out of work-people and give as little, is to have little enough to show by way of good results. To think not of the work alone which the wages claim, but of the man who is to do it; to try one's utmost to make him more of a man for his being employed and to lift up his self-respect, is straightway to increase the value of everything he does, and of the work for which his wages are paid.

The explanation of "dividend or no dividend" is far simpler than it seems, and the New Testament contributes to it. If only a little additional value is placed upon the manhood and womanhood of those employed, and a little increase given to self-respect, responsibility, and conscientiousness where hundreds and thousands are employed, then it requires no great powers of insight to see how rapidly what has hitherto been a failure may become a great commercial success. I attach the greatest importance to the fact that our countrymen in Siberia whom it has been my great privilege to know and make my friends are conducting their great enterprises as honourable and chivalrous men, and have, with public-spirited Russians, like-minded with themselves, laid the foundations of a true Anglo-Russian friendship and agreement. In this I think we are extremely fortunate in the opportunity which world events have brought us, and through no effort of our own. Our own people at home, for the most part, are probably not yet convinced that this is our GOD-given opportunity. I have already freely owned my former prejudices and misconceptions, and explained how quickly they passed away, and I know that others must feel and think as I used to do myself, and that they have had comparatively little as yet to clear their minds, though I trust what is written in these pages may be a help in that direction. But this opportunity which has come to us was possible for Russia's great neighbour at one time, as she was told by one of the most far-seeing men of Europe, but it was carelessly and even contemptuously refused. Great opportunities for great nations never return.

Just as Bismarck pleaded for friendliness with England and against naval expansion for his own country, so also he was quite alive to the possibilities of Russia and its "wonderful materials for making history if it could take the virility of Germany into its national character." The Emperor William, however, differed with his great chancellor upon this as upon other policies he advocated, maintaining that the "Sclavonic peoples are not a nation but only soil out of which a nation with an historic mission may be grown."

We in this country are not as alive to the magnificent opportunity which is now afforded us as are our countrymen in Russia who know its people and its potentialities. And all grades of Russian society, from the Emperor and his Court downwards, also know it, and all who are intelligent in their patriotism desire it. This is what a Russian[14] wrote at the beginning of 1914, when no one was even dreaming of what the close of the year was to see:—

"All progressive Russia is united in desiring a *rapprochement* with England, because there is a universal belief that the influence of English constitutional ideas on Russian internal politics will be most beneficial to the interests of the people and to the general welfare of the country. Being one of the youngest constitutional countries, Russia is holding out a hand of friendship to the mother of all constitutions—England; and she hopes that good relations between them will bear much fruit. This, on the other hand, explains to us why all reactionaries in Russia are so up in arms against the *Entente* with England. There is also a widespread opinion all over Russia that English interests require Russia to be a strong and civilized country with a firmly established constitutional government. If England wishes to have an ally that ally should be a strong one, and Russia cannot be strong so long as reaction is in full swing. The Russian Liberals hope that constant intercourse between the two countries will lead to a better mutual understanding, and will ultimately improve the state of affairs now prevailing in Russia."

Camels at Work—Winter.

France is Russia's ally, and well and faithfully have they both kept the terms of their alliance. We are a new friend only, but it was the British flag the populace demanded, at the beginning of the war, in Petrograd. They went in vast numbers to the British Embassy, and asked for it; and our Ambassador (Sir George Buchanan), though he had only two, handed one of them down, asking them to take care of and return it. They received it with the utmost reverence, bent down and kissed it, as many as could get near, and then, in procession, went cheering and singing through the streets of the capital, the British flag carried high before them.

During the visit of the Fleet earlier in the year to Cronstadt a party of *moujiks* were in a boat within the harbour; and, in their excitement to get near and see all they could of a British warship, they upset their boat, and were thrown struggling into the water. Instantly some twenty of our bluejackets (officers and men) dived amongst them, and in the shortest possible time had them safe in their righted boat again. This made a great impression in Russia, and, though news travels slowly in that vast country, this story went everywhere, continually evoking the comment, "Then it's true, all that we've been told about them—and their *officers* dived in to save the lives of poor peasant folk!" It is a tremendous link between us and them to feel, as they do, that, while claiming all the rights of rank and authority, we feel human ties to be supreme. And just as we read of the British officer early in the war lying wounded in both legs, but lifting himself up with difficulty and crying, "Now *my bonny lads*, shoot straight and let them have it!" so we read of the Russian officer who addresses his men under similar circumstances as "little pigeons"—a special Russian term of endearment. Thus, while there is leadership in the officers of both countries, yet towards their men there is, as boys would say, "no side."

We have only now to read and watch the course of events to keep free from prejudice and suspicion, as we try and discern the signs of the times, and the forces already at work will quite naturally and normally bring the two peoples together in enduring friendship. It is a most significant thing, surely, that three writers so utterly different from each other in their whole outlook upon life as the great surgeon, the popular novelist, and the independent thinker[15] should go to the Holy Land for totally different objects, and *all* find the Russians, above all other nationalities, get very close to their hearts, both for what they were themselves, and for what it was so evidently in them to become.

The most important link of all, however, and that which I have kept in mind in everything I have written, between ourselves and Russia, is that our two races are at heart deeply religious people. The difference between us is that the devout Russian *shows* his religion in every possible way, while the Englishman, with his characteristic reserve, seems to hide it or to speak about it with difficulty. When I was talking last year with a British officer in a specially responsible position, and religion came to be mentioned, he said very shyly and with hesitation, "Well, I have my bit, but I don't talk much about it, though it's everything to me, and I could not live without it." It's "everything" to us and to the Russians, though our public expressions of it are so entirely different. And in Russia once again, as, in former experiences in my episcopal work, I have found that the religious men—when they are the real thing—are all round the best men.

And thus I come to the end, hopefully confident about our relations with the Russians and our work in the world together. This book was asked of me, and pressed upon me at a specially busy and harassing time, and as it has had to be written amidst many distractions and interruptions its imperfections and deficiencies, as I well know, are many, yet it has been a most congenial task to write it. It has been written throughout with the one desire, while giving as true a description of Russia and its people's life as I could, to lead my own countrymen to view them with a friendly eye and a kindly heart. This is essential if we are to have sound and stable relations with each other. Treaties and other diplomatic agreements are indeed mere "scraps of paper" without it, and when the Prime Minister addressed the deputies from the Russian Duma at a luncheon given them in the House of Commons in 1909, he truly and appropriately said that it is not enough to let governments sign treaties and agreements, but the nations themselves must have feelings of friendship for each other, without which all agreements and alliances are not worth the paper on which they are written. I believe—firmly and thankfully I believe it—that our feelings towards those of whom I have written are already those of sympathy and friendship. I am sure it is so in their feelings towards us, and that we are in consequence going to find in

Russia not only a new ally but a very faithful one, and a loyal and true friend for many generations.

FOOTNOTES:

[14] Boris Lebedev, in the February number of the *Russian Review*.

[15] Sir Frederick Treves, Mr. Robert Hichens, and Mr. Stephen Graham.

Milton Keynes UK
Ingram Content Group UK Ltd.
UKHW011102080324
439029UK00005B/396